A *in the* DESERT

OSIANDER ROSE

Copyright © 2023 by Osiander Rose.

All rights reserved. No part of this publication may be reproduced, distributed, or transmitted in any form or by any means, including photocopying, recording, or other electronic or mechanical methods, without the prior written permission of the author, except in the case of brief quotations embodied in critical reviews and certain other noncommercial uses permitted by copyright law.

This work is a combination of biblical scripture interpretations and the author's personal experiences. Unless otherwise indicated, the scripture interpretations are simply that: an opinionated interpretation and should not be viewed as religious doctrine. The events and names are not in any way related to or have bearing on real life events of the readers. An initial apology for those who feel their personal experiences are dictated in some form. All stories have no bearing, on the general population of readers. All names were personally created by the author and have no bearing or resemblance to the general public.

Printed in the United States of America.

Library of Congress Control Number: 2023930247

ISBN	Paperback	979-8-88887-126-3
	eBook	979-8-88887-127-0

Westwood Books Publishing LLC
Atlanta Financial Center
3343 Peachtree Rd NE Ste 145-725
Atlanta, GA 30326

www.westwoodbookspublishing.com

OTHER BOOKS BY THE AUTHOR

God, Where Are My Muscles?
Preaching to the Tenth Pew: What I Heard the Word Say to Me series
- Book 1: *In the Early Years*
- Book 2: *Coming Face to Face with God*
- Book 3: *The Holy Ghost will Guide You*
- Book 4: *The Difference a Day Makes*

Trials to Triumph: God Always Has a Plan
Choose Your Weapon Choose Your Side

To order books on online: access the author's website at: https://authorosianderrose.com/

Use the author's QR code

DEDICATION

This book is dedicated to all of the fallen and surviving troops of Operation Enduring Freedom, Operation Iraqi Freedom I, II and III, those Americans who continue to fight the war on terrorism and any conflicts for American freedom. They built boats in America's deserts, not knowing the end state. Like, Noah, we are instructed to build even when we can't see the God's purpose. There is a purpose in our lives and God will bless us in the end. Build your boat and keep your power connected to the power source of Christ. Live every day as if it all matters today. When you get to heaven, you will know then why the boat in the desert was necessary. You will then remember every blessing God gave you and every victory won during your time on earth.

May God continue to richly bless you

Preview

Colossians 4:5-6…be wise and make most of every opportunity. Let your words be full of grace.

Luke 19:41-44…had you only known that this day would bring you peace. But you didn't know it was a sign of God coming to you.

Jesus said to us, "It is Me."

I fazed out of my reflective state to hear the Army preacher continue with her sermon. I was so involved in my reflection that I forgot about the golden shoes. There stood the preacher on the floor just below the pulpit. I raised my head to the level of her boots. I screamed out loud when I saw the golden boots setting at my eye level. I was sure someone heard my scream.

It startled me! I looked to my left and my right. No one appeared alarmed or frazzled. The boots were fiery golden and I was sure I wasn't the only one who saw them. I wasn't ready to see the symbol. I couldn't figure out its meaning. A floating preacher and a set of golden shoes worn by the divine elite; I was ready for my time.

The sermon!

There's a purpose, a season, a time for everything. The devil wants us to focus on the calamities of the world. Don't let him win your heart and steal your soul. Remember God is overseeing the events of our lives. Stay focused on God's works.

Regardless of the reflection of today's sermon, I still wasn't ready. I understood. I just didn't feel like I was ready.

We arrived at my new place. The same soldiers helped me to unload all of my equipment. I had unconsciously packed a few of my senior soldier's videos. I promised myself to give them back later. I had more gear than I'd originally thought. Nonetheless I sadly unloaded the vehicle and placed it in my new surroundings. I was going to count the number of trips to and from the vehicle. It wasn't helping me to feel better.

I cried inside knowing that this was my time, season and purpose. I choked on my words. I wanted to ask "why?" I told myself that this was a new beginning. I was in the process of taking every opportunity to get closer to God and make every effort to understand the will of my Father, God. And of course, along with His perfect plan.

I walked in the gravel and sand to get another handful of my things. I would organize it later. Some of the stuff I had really didn't get used. Much of the stuff I needed I didn't have. My time, season and purpose. I didn't see it coming. I made six more trips to and from the vehicle. The soldiers drove away leaving me to start fresh in the morning greeting a new unit.

"Don't hold on to the way things used to be. Don't resist transition. Stay focused and connected. Stay on track for redemption. Don't hold fast to old stuff."

I found the card with the Colonel's phone number and office number. I was slightly familiar with the lay out of the new installation. I decided to ask directions from the first soldier I passed if I started heading in the wrong direction. I always made plenty of time to get where I needed to go. So, I planned to walk slowly in order to take in my new surroundings.

I stood in the middle of my new residence missing my own camp. I missed the unpredictability of the sand storms and the daily malfunctions of the air conditioners and shower points not having sufficient water. Walking through the neighborhood of the new installation made me laugh about the times I would get ready for a shower and there was no water. I'd have to use a few water bottles or wait it out until the afternoon. It was the desert so who cared?

I laughed out loud also when I thought about how everyone came flying out of the tents one afternoon when the air conditioner went out. If we needed to call an emergency formation all we had to do was shut off the air conditioner and you'd see hundreds of troops out front. I also ate a lot of sand at my old camp. I couldn't wear my cocoa butter skin cream or chap stick. If I did wear it, sand would get stuck on my lips and face. I just never knew when a storm was coming so I had to carry my scarf and stay ready. Those small things in retrospect were actually pretty funny and all of a sudden, I realized that I liked them.

Now, I had to let go of those memories and put some focus on my new job. Morning for me would come quick. I returned to my room and began sorting my things.

Don't hold on to the way things used to be. Move on and accept the transition. My new job; whatever that might be.

"Turn your Bibles please to Matthew 24:36-39." The pause was natural and it gave us time to find the scripture. "These scriptures or verses, if you may, tell you why you shouldn't hold on to old things. The way things used to be. The way you want things to be in *your* mind. Matthew 24:36-39 tells us that no one knows when the time and season is over. Not even the angels in heaven."

That was a bit of a relief. I used to think that God had a plan so perfect and secret and we (the humans) were the only ones who knew nothing about it. I now know that God's *own* angels didn't even know. Sometimes it's just not good for everybody to know everything.

"Do you have a few words to say?" The Commander stood next to me and waited for me to finish my few words.

"I am honored," I begin in my most professional tone, "that the United States Army has found great valor, honor and entrusted me with a higher rank to continue serving my country. To continue to mold soldiers like you into soldiers like myself. The Army has also seen fit to give you a greater challenge to mold me into the best officer the Army has to offer." I smiled and motioned that my speech was done. I didn't have much to say. I was happy about my promotion, just not real wordy about it. Then it was the Commander's turn to speak. He stepped in front of me. I took a few steps back to give him space. He put the unit at ease and began his speech.

"Good morning to all of you. I am indeed honored to award this fine soldier a rank of greater responsibility. She is doing a fine job and we wish her well." He paused and the unit readied to applaud but he wasn't quite finished with his speech. He took a deep breath and continued.

About the Author

Osiander Rose is a dynamic writer. She has grown even more in Christ. She writes about her understanding of God's perfect plan in a way for all levels of Christianity to understand. Take time to read *Preaching to the Tenth Pew* books 1-4, *God, Where Are My Muscles?*, *Trials to Triumph*, *Choose Your Weapon Choose Your Side* and enjoy this one: *A Boat in the Desert*. You'd be amazed to know how good God is and how much He truly loves His people.

Osiander Rose is going places and she has a testimony to tell. You'll love her and the words she puts to paper.

Untitled

There stood a military Chaplain devoted to preach God's Word. Downed with heavy rank and a pressed uniform. Who'd ever heard?

I never ever saw one bring the Word of Truth to soldiers young and old. Preaching powerful sermons from the pulpit. Good enough to be retold. The very first message filled my soul. There's a time, a purpose, a season for everything we do. The second sermon told us how we can stay on track to help us make it through.

Listen…

There's a purpose, a season, a time for everything. God is overseeing it all; all the events of our life. Hence there's no need to worry, don't stress or fret. You may feel terrible now but wait because your time just isn't over yet. There's a time, a season, a purpose. Stay focused on God's work. Stand still and listen for what the Holy Spirit has to say. Be ready for God's voice to tell you the actions you must take. For the devil is among us. His job is to tear us down. He wants our attention on the gloomy situations of the way things would and used to be. His presence is simple: Aid us in wading in our world of sinful calamities. But we can't get stuck on "why, why, why?" We have to remember that God is…sensitive, merciful, and knows our very disposition. In the end He has a much better position for our current condition.

There's a purpose, a time, a season for everything we do. Don't waste moments of your life when it ain't even your time to go through. Instead commit yourself to ministering to others the goodness God provides. If nothing else remind them that for their very life Christ died. Think about your own trials and your blade level experiencing. At least you can go through your sufferings as a human being. Christ was beaten, spit on, and belittled for our helpless sake. Now why would God do all that and make you go through stuff and burden you with things He knows you can't take? Stay on track. Wait for your redemption. Jesus died to deliver us from the stuff our brethren did to Him. His blood was shed for us all and for all of us He'd do it all again. Stay focused and connected.

Pray for wisdom and perspective on your situation. We can't always control others' actions but at least we can control ours thru meditation. Don't worry, fret or stress on things God is putting you through. It may just be the appointed time and very purpose and the season for you. Remember when your season comes, a host of people want to lend their support. Just cry out in your voice. "Sir, I would see Jesus for this report." Trials are flooding in your life and all and everything seems useless. Cry out in your voice. "Sir, I would see Jesus." Your blade size situation is rising above the bush. Cry out in your voice. "Sir, I would see Jesus." You're trying hard to make it but your neck's all caught in a noose. Cry out in your voice. "Sir, I would see Jesus." When you're experiencing heartache and your spirit is going to burst. Cry out in your voice. "Sir, I would see Jesus." When your friends and love ones leave you and you feel you've lost their touch. Cry out in your voice. "Sir, I would see Jesus." When you worry about your calling and your mind is filled with confusion. Cry out in your voice. "Sir, I would see Jesus." When finances hit rock bottom. Bills have to be paid. They must. Cry out in your voice. "Sir, I would see Jesus." You are stricken with an illness for which there is no cure. Cry out in your voice. "Sir, I would see Jesus." There will always be something with a purpose, a time, and a season. No man knows, not even God's angels, the who, the when, or the reason.

But…

At the times you go through stuff and you can't see where it will finally end cry out and leave it there. Don't go back and pick it up again. Claim. Sir, I've given that to Jesus. Then wait because…God's tomorrow is like your future but many, many years to come. His today is a thousand precious years but all wrapped into your day one.

So, no matter what you go through at your appointed purpose, season, and time,

Remember God is standing right there to provide you with strength and peace of mind.

OSIANDER ROSE copyright 2004

Prologue

The night was long but Coriander was determined not to attend church with the transportation sergeant. It was the third time he'd invited her and the third time she wanted to tell him no. She couldn't bring herself to attending another church after blaming God for separating her from her family under such short notice.

"How could He do this Motivator? I thought He loved us. We've never been apart like this before. What if you don't love me when I get back? What if our children don't remember me? What if something terrible happens? I thought I understood and was working on my misunderstandings and my short falls. I guess I only understand when things are like I want them or when I can see the end state up front."

The Motivator stood near the staircase. He checked his watch to make sure there was still time to pick up the boys. The year had been a happy one. Now Coriander was losing ground. She'd received notice to serve. She felt like Noah when God told him to build a boat. He was in the desert! She played the scenario in her mind...

"Noah, I need for you to build a boat and identify a male and female of each animal to go on the boat. Tell the people that a terrible flood will wipe out all mankind. They need to believe and help build the boat."

"But God, we're in the desert. It never rains in the desert my Lord."

"It will rain soon Noah and I need for you to be prepared. And be sure and tell the people to help and be watchful of the day."

"I'll do my best Lord." Noah believed and trusted God. He told the people what God said.

The people laughed and made fun of him. But Noah's family was afraid of what God could and will do. They helped Noah build the boat as God instructed.

"We will build as you command my Lord. We will build and occupy as you commanded."

For years Noah and his family built the boat for those same years the people laughed and teased them.

"I thought you said it was going to rain. I don't see any rain. It's never rained in the desert you idiot!" And the people laughed.

"It's been years Noah and there's still no rain. How could you have believed what God said to you?"

"You trying to get us all scared and all and there hasn't been a thought of rain for fifteen years Noah." And the people laughed.

The years came and went. Decades passed and Noah held on to what God told him.

A boat in the desert. Noah was building a boat in the desert because God had a plan. Another plan of God's that was scores of years away yet, Noah trusted God. Without fail, Noah trusted God and continued building the boat a top of sand and believing every day, any day rain would come.

After all those years Noah finally…

Coriander fished for a legitimate reason for not going to church with the sergeant. She replayed the conversation over and over in her mind. He was absolutely polite and he meant well spiritually.

"I just can't take another sermon right now Clay. I thought after examining myself, I found all the answers and now this. I'm away from home after all that hard work trying to figure out what God wants from me."

Coriander took her pouting stances. Clay laughed. She watched his hazel brown eyes dance in the coolness of the evening. His uniform was wrinkled from driving all day.

Clay touched Coriander's shoulder, "you won't ever get all the answers. I don't know all the answers myself. I don't even want to know the answers. After watching Bruce Almighty, I really don't want to know the answers and I sure as yellow don't want to have God's job for a day. I thought being president was bad. No girl, being God is worst."

"I'm really busy tomorrow, Clay. I'll think about it but I think we're going to be working or having class. We only have a few weeks left before we have to leave."

Coriander poked at her own uniform. She usually talks eye to eye but her eyes traveled. She knew Clay wasn't buying the "I got to work" piece. Coriander tried to think of more to say.

"Coriander, I mean this. I'm going to be right here where I'm dropping you off tomorrow at 1000 hours. Please be here girl. No if ands or buts. I know you out rank me but when it comes to God there's no rank. So tomorrow, here, 1000 hours no excuses. You'll love me for it later. Now that is one promise I can make."

Clay went to the driver's cab and pulled the handle to let Coriander out.

"See you tomorrow girl."

Coriander exited the bus. She clutched the straps of her book bag. She waved at the bus as Clay pulled off to his next stop. The night air woke her. She prayed as she went into her barracks. This is like that boat in the desert. All that preparation and no one can't even see the rain. The barracks door slammed. Coriander jumped.

She was about to begin another spiritual adventure trying to discern the times for a season and begin a journey that didn't make sense to her right then. An umbrella goes up when it rains, gloves are pulled out and worn when the winter weather is bad, and food is prepared and eaten at the first pains of hunger. These thoughts rolled around in her head for a few moments. She fished hard for an excuse.

"Why go to church all the time if you haven't gotten what you need from it yet? Why contaminate what I already have? I'm not ready for any more floating preachers and reasons for actions and reactions."

Why would a boat be needed in the desert?

Coriander paused short of her barracks door to think about, what seemed to be just a moment in time, how her seventh pew adventure began when…

Chapter One

SURVIVING A SATANIC ATTACK

I stood at the bus stop waiting for Clay. I knew he'd probably be running late because he lived far away from my barracks and he had to get on post. I picked at my hair and dress. I didn't know why I was nervous and excited too. I knew that God loved me and wanted only the best for me. I also couldn't see myself waiting forever for a miracle. The bus pulled up. I laughed. I was sure we'd go to church in a personal vehicle. We were going to church in the post bus. I laughed and got in.

"Don't say it, Clay. I know what you're going to say so don't." I straightened my dress and clutched my book bag close.

"And what was I going to say?" Clay was a medium height young sergeant. He spent several years in the Marine Corps before transferring into the Army. He was a confident young man and full of motivation. I watched his hazel eyes dance as he waited for the answer to his question and kept his eyes on the road. "And what was I going to say?" He had a heavy southern accent. I hadn't asked him too many questions about his past. I thought I'd do that today during the ride to church.

"I thought you were going to say glad you came or good thinking about it or something like that."

"Oh no. I just wanted to have someone to ride with me. I figured since you're off on Sunday then we could go together. Plus, I like your company and I don't think you've been off the post since you've been here. And have you been to church since you've been here? Don't answer that question." Clay kept his eyes on the road. He smiled beautifully and his southern accent made me laugh to myself. He was indeed a gentleman. I appreciated the fact that he had an added interest in me attending church. I hadn't been off the post since I got to the base. When I was at home, I always enjoyed going to church. I didn't feel like fighting the devil so I decided in the middle of the night to be ready for the ride.

A young lady was standing in the pulpit reading the announcements. She spoke perfectly. I listened attentively. It wasn't like I was going to be able to attend some or any of the functions. Some of them I wish I could attend. At the end of the announcements, she asked for all first-time visitors to please stand. I didn't. Why didn't I stand? I couldn't remember but I'm sure it was because I never feel like a visitor in church. I'm not sure if that was being selfish on my part or rude. I didn't want to make any enemies on the first Sunday. Funny I should think that. The sermon was telling me how I could survive a satanic attack. How could I survive an attack on my spirit? Maybe that's what kept me in my seat.

Pastor Jernell L. Adames stood in the pulpit with a smile on his face. He motioned for the announcement clerk to read a final announcement then she took her seat. I watched the clerk return to her seat with grace. Must be an important position I thought. Telling what will happen next in the good Word of God. Pastor Adames was about six feet tall, slim and well dressed. It was hot yet his double-breasted wool looking suit made him look like a devoted preacher. There was no sweat on his face. He looked refreshed and ready to rightly divide the Word of truth. I wasn't sure if I should take notes or listen. His face gave me the impression that God indeed had a word for me today. I suddenly felt joy knowing that God loves me. He truly loves me. A hot breeze crossed my face…

"We always ask for others to pray for us. We place our names on the pray for list. We solicit the prayers of the saints. We steadily converse with God to protect us from the devil. We do all of that. Why?" Pastor Adames paused as if he was waiting for an answer from the congregation. His cream skin and deep voice pressed through the congregation leaving an impression of hope on the people. The air suddenly tightened around me. I was frightened. God was coming for me right in the middle of service. I gasped. I looked about myself. The people went about as if nothing was going on in my area. I wasn't sure if I was ready for all the commotion. I quickly counted the pews. I was sitting in the seventh pew. Number seven, God's number. I knew then that this would be an adventure.

"Turn your bibles if you would please to Ephesians the sixth chapter. We will begin reading at the eleventh verse." Pastor Adames paused. I could hear the crisp pages turning. I pulled out my bible and quickly turned to the said chapter and verse. The pages stopped. The pastor spoke. "You will never find anyone who loves you more than Jesus loves you. You just won't. I thought you all should know that before I get into the real lesson for today."

The quietness of the congregation made me more fearful. I still felt that breeze around me. It was a hot day. I looked around. Everyone was sweating or fanning. What was really taking place at this church?

Pastor Adames swayed and pursed his lips. The bulge of his small belly made a print on the front of his suit. I noticed it when he stepped away from the pulpit. I guess we all have something we don't care to have. From behind the pulpit, he appeared strong, confident, near physical perfection. The little bulge let me know that there was work to do. I had some work to do myself. Perhaps a late-night snack was working against Pastor Adames and an evil spirit was working against me. What could I do?

"How to Survive a Satanic Attack. You are going to survive any attack on you from Satan. The devil's job is to make our lives miserable. He gets up and goes to work as we do. He makes sure we have an enemy. We all have an enemy. Every day the devil is attacking somebody's life. That's his full-time job!"

"I never looked at it that way!" I'm sure the saint that was sitting on my left and right heard me. I know Clay did because he started laughing. He sat on my immediate left. The devil's job is to make my life miserable. He has a full-time job. Not a relief but a nightmare. I watched Pastor Adames move back behind the podium. He touched his Bible and continued. I assumed he had no script. His lips pursed and he pressed his side jacket pockets. The pause was killing me.

"Tell it preacher," a voice shouted from the congregation.

"Amen!" Several spiritual accolades went about the church. After they died down a bit Pastor Adames continued.

"On your job you work for so many hours and then you take a small break. As a matter-of-fact you take at least two breaks and a lunch when you're at work. And some of us go to work and break all day!" The pastor paused to take in the friendly comments that doused the church. Some members were laughing.

They were comical which seemed to set the members at ease. I just wanted to know how I could survive an attack from Satan. Since no one could tell me how to make the enemy on ground disappear I figured if I know how to survive a satanic attack then I'd be well ahead of the game. I listened to the last of the praise comments.

"Sometimes I don't get a break at all!"

"Tell it pastor!"

"That's right preacher."

"Amen, amen!"

"Don't tell it all today!"

It was indeed a joyous day in general. I tried not to be so serious about the sermon. I relaxed and watched the words fall from the pastor's lips.

"The devil on the other hand isn't going to give you a break. He doesn't take breaks so you won't get a break from him. He stays in the business of placing struggles and obstacles in your path. He strives on making your life feel like you've built a boat in the desert. What are you waiting for, rain? Not in the desert my dear saints. Definitely not in the desert."

I had to pull out my notebook. I opened it up to a clean page. I listened careful to the pastor as I counted the pews once more. I was sitting on the seventh pew. A Seventh Pew Spiritual Adventure I wrote at the top of the clean page. I smiled and wrote A Boat in the Desert.

The night air slapped my face again and again. I wanted to be sure I wasn't hearing the voices of ghosts. I moved toward the house hoping to only see three children under the age of ten years old. I wasn't even looking for the Motivator. I rehearsed my prayer.

"Lord please help my daughter find a good job. She will do so much better if she has a really well-paying job. With a well-paying job she could buy a nice house and live comfortably. I know she's still young but she's ready to take on the world. She is ready. Amen Lord. I'm still waiting patiently. Amen"

I walked up to the front door. I could see the figure through the side window on the door. As I entered, I confirmed. There was my daughter cooking. Mylene is my oldest daughter. She looks just like her dad, the Motivator. At age seventeen and a half, she looked almost grown. She stood over the stove stirring what I assumed was spaghetti. For a few seconds I watched the ceremony of her hand and blouse sleeve stir the contents of the pot. She stood on her tiptoes. She looked cute. I smiled a bit. I glanced around the kitchen to see what else was going to be served with the spaghetti. I didn't see anything else. Just spaghetti I thought.

Mylene was fairly busy so I made no verbal or nonverbal interruptions. I didn't need to count the children. I was sure there were still six of them floating about the house. I went to the restroom down stairs feeling slightly discouraged. I wasn't sure if I should have repeated my prayer. I didn't think I needed to. I had asked God for something and things were still the same. Maybe I wasn't ready. What more did I need to do? My "eighteen ninety plan" was to go into effect in two months. When you turn eighteen you have ninety days to secure an adult life. I had to force myself to just wait and be in position to receive the answer to my prayer. Why had I made all that preparation if God wasn't going to show me, I mean us the path? My mind had wondered. Now I was returning to the present sermon.

"That's right pastor. That's right." The big hat lady in front of me waved her small hands. She was feeling righteous this morning. She made me feel good as well. I smiled and made certain to listen closely. There had to be a word from the Lord somewhere. I jotted a few notes and wondered once more.

"Dinner's ready guys. I watched five children come out of various rooms of the house. Yep, they're all here. Still. I wondered a bit knowing this was not the time. They must have read it. I could see the expression of their faces as they dug into the spaghetti sprawled across the plastic plate. I was about to bring it to everyone's attention right before the cornbread graced the table. I had my mind all made up that there was only spaghetti that I didn't even smell the cornbread. I'm usually good about smells and other things. I was disappointed in myself. The plan was prepared and I missed the time of execution.

My oldest daughter smiled at her sisters and brothers as she shouted, "Dinner is served!"

I was the only one caught off guard.

"Saints of God, turn with me to Ephesians the sixth chapter beginning at the eleventh verse. Say Amen when you have it."

I flipped through the pages of my palm sized bible that my mother had given to me to take on my deployment. I licked my fingers to turn the last pages to the said chapter.

"Put on the full armor of God so that you are ready to stand against any evil that confronts you. Remember the devil will not give you a break. He has nothing else to do except hound you to turn against God. At five o'clock, I get off work. I take off my work clothes and put on comfortable clothes and walk around the house. But the devil is *still* at work. He continuously roams to and from seeking whom he can devour. The devil is attacking somebody's life right now! So put on the whole armor of God!"

The pastor took in a deep breath. I watched him unbutton his wool like suit. I know his suit had to be expensive. He wore a French cut dress shirt. The masculine pink went well with the metal gray.

"Yes, the devil is attacking but you can survive that satanic attack. Put on the whole armor of God for our trial is not with flesh and blood but against the rules, authorities, and power of darkness and spiritual forces of evil. But you can have victory over such. Victory is already claimed. You already got a way out. The struggle against the devil is like a fixed fight. We know who's going to win. Therefore, put the whole armor on. God tells us we can survive. We're the ones who say we can't."

The pastor was right. Every time something comes about, we have a meeting to discuss what we can't do to not get the task done. Whoever took the time to think about what we can do and get the task done? I readjusted my seating and placed my attention back on the sermon. I was definitely getting a good word from the Lord.

"Victory saints. Victory is already ours. Let's take a look at the story of Job. Job was a real fighter in his day. I'm sure I would have thrown in my towel at the first tragedy. I know many of you would have done the same."

"That's right pastor!"

"Tell 'em preacher!"

I laughed because the praise comments and the pastor's statements were true. I know I would have given up on the first go.

I watched the children eat the spaghetti. The cornbread did smell good. I hated myself for not smelling it the first time. In my haste I had missed the smell of cornbread. I wanted to argue with God because He hadn't come through for me today. I didn't feel like waiting. I wanted my victory right away. My eighteen ninety plan was fading. My daughter would soon be eighteen and no company had yet to contact her for an interview.

I heard the Motivator come inside.

"I smell dinner. Love, are you cooking or did Mylene cook?" The dry sweat made his face look partially white. He passed by the downstairs restroom. I immediately pointed for him to wash his hands and change clothes. He smiled and went on his way. Minutes later he graced to greet the children and their partially finished dinner. I stayed in the dining room. I wasn't ready to take on the fact that my prayer had gone unanswered today. I thought of all the things my daughter wouldn't be able to accomplish while she stood in the kitchen bragging about her dinner and serving her siblings instead of preparing for an important interview. From my vantage point, see that the other children each wore a spaghetti smile. They didn't seem worried about my worry. My life was on the edge of being miserably disappointing. I guess I was the one taking it in that direction.

The pastor's voice didn't fade or flinch. He began speaking calmly retelling the story of Job. My heart fluttered. I set my pen to the side. I knew I'd remember this without writing it down.

"Job was an upright man. If I could get away with it saints, I'd say Job was God's favorite. You know when you have a favorite child. Now we're not supposed to say that but there are tell-tell signs of a favorite employee, a favorite child, a favorite student, a favorite sister and such. We brag about everything they do. They can never do wrong and we light up like a Roman candle when they're around. Job was sort of God's favorite. God knew Job trusted Him and thought the heaven and earth of Him."

Pastor Adames bit his lower lip and stared at what I think were the pages of his sermon. The congregation waited those few seconds. The seconds felt like days to me. My mind began to wonder but I caught myself. I praised my efforts. The praise comments drowned out the silence. I shuffled in my sit and continued my attention. I almost forgot that Clay was sitting next to me. He had said almost nothing for some time. I tossed a weak smile his way. The pastor spoke.

"The devil even knew Job was faithful. He knew God had blessed Job tremendously. Job had thousands of everything. It's like Job had twenty-five Mercedes Benzes, nine Cadillacs, 4 Teslas, six mansion, sixteen children, all living and making great money, twenty-five grandchildren, a beautiful wife that resembled Halle Berry, even after having all those children…"

Laughter plastered the walls of the church. Many of the congregation could relate. I certainly would have loved to have a third of what Job had if I were in his day and a fraction of what the pastor just spouted out. Life was surely good for them but I'm sure drama came with it. Plus, I'd want to look more like Jennifer Lopez than Halle Berry.

"God was a blessing to them a thousand times over. God loved Job and his family. But the devil, who never takes a lunch break, never takes a day off, doesn't go on vacation, wanted to prove a point to God. He wanted to prove that there is no man that God created who could survive a satanic attack. He was sure there was no one." Pastor Adames removed his suit coat. The pastor's aide snapped up and gracefully received the coat. She placed it neatly on the back of her chair. I could see her sitting erect as to not wrinkle it. At the rate the pastor was rolling, I didn't think he minded it much. I redirected my focus on the pastor's words. I watched the sweat form on the front of his masculine pink shirt. He shuffled a few pages and decided against using them.

"So, God allowed, listen to me saints, God permitted the devil to rough up Job. He permitted him to deadline a few of those Benzes, kill off a few children, and inflict a bunch of those grandbabies. God permitted the devil to make Job sick. God allowed all of that to happen. Now Job was like, *"What'd I do to deserve this? Why am I being kicked to the curb? What's up Lord? We ain't kickin' it no more? I'm not your favorite anymore? Tell a brother something! This is bad."* Job didn't know what to do about the sudden death of more than half his cattle. In today's time, I could see Job being laid off his six-figure job with that first digit being a two. But Job took it like a man! He took it all like a real Christian. And God was smiling on Job. He was proud of Job. Job found favor in God's grace…."

I began to laugh out loud. Clay stared at me. He leaned over and whispered, "Why are you laughing Coriander? This is a serious sermon." Clay had sweat droplets on his forehead. "Coriander." He wanted to raise his voice but he kept calling my name in his strained whisper. He sounded funny using my first name. I didn't usually let soldiers use my first name. I was laughing so hard I didn't mind at the time. I tried to speak. I choked on my words as my laughter spilled into the pew in front of us. The member on my right scooted over. I guess she was a bit embarrassed. I kept laughing.

"Now saints, if that was you…"

I burst into laughter. I imagined a dominating female or an arrogant male talking to God. I imagined that person telling God how much he or she needed to praise Him in style. The more I thought about Pastor Adames using Job's situation in today's time, the more I laughed. My sides began to ache. Clay grabbed my forearm and escorted me into the vestibule. I tried to speak again but the laughter got caught in my throat. I could still hear Pastor Adames above my laughter.

"We see people everyday wanting everything and working for nothing. We see people everyday acting like somebody owes them something. Then when all their stuff is gone then they want to blame it all on God by reminding Him of how good He's supposed to be to us."

I wiped my face and held onto Clay. He was trying not to laugh. I could still hear Pastor Adames' voice penetrating the vestibule doors.

"Now saints you know if that was you, you'd rip the church walls down! You would be the first one telling God how much you prayed and how many times you went to church and how you paid your tithes every week. You would be the one reminding God about how you helped Sista Sally and Cousin Jo-Jo get off welfare. You would tell it all to God in attempts to justify why He should take nothing from you."

The congregation roared with praise comments. I was still laughing a little but not enough to keep me from hearing the pastor's words and understand his point. And you know something, he was absolutely right.

Minutes later the church was quiet. The last syllable fell upon the church carpet. The pastor paced the pulpit for a few seconds. He wanted to make sure we were soaking it all in. I watched him pace back and forth for the third time. On the fourth pace, I returned to my seat with Clay. When we sat down, he whispered, "Girl you a fool. I better be quiet before you let loose again." He smiled and patted my knee. I calmed to listen to the rest of this terrific sermon. I was glad I came. It was a real treat for me.

"The devil is busy I tell you. He was busy with Job. Had God not told him to stop he would have just kept on Job. The devil don't take a break. Ask you to do something after five o'clock, your response would be, "Chile I just got off work!" or "Girl, I'm tired." But the devil, he ain't ever tired. He will get off one job and report to the next. He flawlessly works two ends against the middle. He stays on the job."

The pastor took a few moments to wipe his forehead. Before his handkerchief touched the podium the pastor's aide was there ready to pick it up and replace it with a fresh one. Smooth. She was ready at all times. You couldn't slip an ant by her. I wrote a few of the sentences in my notebook. I wanted to remember this sermon. It was on fire. The congregation shouted out more praise comments. Pastor Adames smiled and continued.

"I told you that there is a way to survive a satanic attack"

"Tell us how," a voice shouted from the congregation.

"Yeah preacher, please tell us how."

I leaned toward Clay, "Please tell me how." I readied my pen and paper.

The pastor took a few breaths. He must have felt the congregation relax. I'm sure there were a few others who really needed this word from God today. I for one did.

From watching the children, dinner was a hit. The Motivator wasn't a good candidate for evaluating meals. He just ate without complaint. He made life simple. Live and serve Christ. How much simpler can you get than that. I waited for Mylene to finish cleaning the kitchen. I selfishly refused to help. I don't think I even ate dinner. The Motivator would discuss my actions later. I should have eaten. But I didn't. That showed a bad example for the family. I'm sure there was inquiry about my presence. I always told my children that our home was a safe haven. I demanded they not bring trash off the street into our home. We need our home to wind down I told them. Now here I was building a potential barrier in our home.

Mylene dried the last dish and placed it in the cabinet. She was heading out of the kitchen.

"Mylene," I called out to her. I could hear my voice crack at the sound of her name. That wasn't fair. She turned immediately and came to me. I watched her eyes dance knowing the family was pleased with her accomplishment. She wasn't even concerned that I may have been a little stand offish. She sat on the couch where I stood. She wiped her hands that smelled of detergent.

Before I spoke again, she said, "I saved you some dinner. Those boys were really hungry. I didn't make a lot of spaghetti but I was sure to save you a few extra pieces of cornbread. I know how you love cornbread."

She laughed and I was supposed to at least smile. I strained one for good measure.

"Mylene, have you thought about what you're going to do?"

"When?" I could have screamed. My face probably did.

"When you turn eighteen. You know you'll be grown by then and you'll have to find you your own way. Remember the agreement, you have four years and I have four years once you get into high school. We've been at this every day for four years. You've graduated from high school and in a couple months you'll be an adult." I wished the Motivator was having this conversation. He didn't because it was my plan, not our plan.

Mylene's smile faded. I didn't like that. I always want to see smiles on my children's face. The fading seemed to make the dinner she'd prepared go up as a vapor in the wind. I should've thought about my timing. Adult life was much more complicated than a pot of spaghetti and a pan of cornbread. And that wasn't at all fair to think or say out loud. Something else was done before that even came about. I forced myself to have no pity. Someone would call. We'd sent out over five resumes and six college applications.

"I haven't really thought about it much. The truth is I don't think I'm ready. I don't even know what to do or where to begin." The dance in her eyes faded as her face sunk. I looked at her and fear came into my heart. She isn't ready for this cruel world and I'm about to send her out there to fight. With what?

"What is it Mylene?" I rubbed my hands together to keep from placing them on my hips.

"How can I make it in the world?"

I brought my attention back to the sermon. The pastor was still wiping his forehead. I could feel the tension of the congregation as they readied to hear the ways to survive a satanic attack.

"There are two ways to surviving a satanic attack. The first step is to identify the enemy. Turn back with me to Ephesians six and take a look at verse twelve."

The Bible pages shuffled and the pastor waited a few moments.

"When you have it again, say Amen."

After several "amens", the pastor continued. "Our struggle is not against flesh and blood. Saints the attacks on us from Satan are not earthly battles. The Bible says we are fighting against the rulers, the authorities and powers of the dark world and against spiritual forces of evil. It didn't say that we are fighting against Sista Morgan or Brother

Matthews. They're *not* the enemy. Saints we need to know who the enemy is in order to survive the attack."

The praise comments were weak. I assumed the members were half expecting another kind of enemy. But it's all true. Sometimes we don't even know who the enemy is and according to this preacher it's the same enemy all the time. Satan. He moves about seeking who he can destroy and if we don't know that he's the enemy then we have placed our defenses elsewhere and then baam he's in our hearts and souls! I thought about my daughter. I was making her to be the enemy. She wasn't the enemy. The devil working through the people of the world was the enemy that would make her life a constant struggle. Put fear of adulthood in her. I knew then that I'd have to change the way I prepared her to face the world. I failed. I hadn't given her some armor.

"Saints the devil will never leave you alone. Even though God gave you the armor, the devil still stays on his job. You have to know that the enemy isn't us. The enemy is the evil spirits of the world. Don't get mad at Brother Rice because it ain't Brother Rice's doing, it is the devil working in him. The first step in surviving a satanic attack is to know the enemy."

That was easy to do. So, I thought. We are all afflicted and challenged by the spirits of the world. But instead of trying those spirits by the spirit we lash out at the human who we think is responsible for our strife. Pastor Adames says no. We are not wrestling against flesh and blood. Mylene told me she wasn't ready for the world and she was right. She wasn't ready for the world but the devil was good and ready for her.

"Put on the whole armor of God so that you can stand firm against the devil's work!" That was the voice of Pastor Adames. I looked at Clay. I must have been startled out of my daydream. I checked my notes. I was still on track.

"Put on the whole armor of God so that you are able to stand your ground. And even after everything is said and done, still stand. The devil will come at you, remember he doesn't take vacation, every time he knows you're weak. You have to keep on your armor and stand."

What happened to Job? Where was his armor? I placed my hand on Clay's knee. I knew this wasn't bible class. Clay glanced in my direction and then returned his attention to the pastor. The pastor was wiping his forehead. He made a gesture and adjusted the tie on his shirt.

"Saints, I told you there are two steps in surviving a satanic attack. Being able to identify the enemy is one and the second one is to stand firm against the satanic forces."

The pastor walked in front of the podium. He had a look of confidence painted on his face.

I was asking myself, "How do I stand against the forces?" I know I had to put on the whole armor and after it's on what do I do next? I watched Pastor Adames as he graced the floor to continue. He was still sweaty but his shirt still appeared neat and intact. The gray wool looking pants held its leg creases. It was only then I noticed the pastor was wearing golden shoes. I thought it rather odd. I watched the golden shoes almost glide across the floor and seamlessly returned to his original position behind the podium. It was hot in the church and many of the members were vigorously fanning themselves and their children. But the pastor was calm looking. He was sweating but he was still strapped sharp. I gasped and stared all at the same time. My mouth was probably wide open. I had flash backs of my angelical preacher experience. I wasn't sure if I was ready to go down that road. Just to be sure, I leaned over to Clay.

"Clay, why does he have on those bright golden shoes with a metal gray suit?"

I held my breath hoping for what I wanted to hear. I felt sweat coming out of the pores of my palms. I stared at the pastor. His lips were moving but I couldn't hear his words. I grew anxious because it seemed like eternity before Clay responded.

"His shoes aren't gold, they're a dark color. You should get your eyes checked or take off those glasses."

I wanted to tell him to look again but was afraid he'd think I was crazy. The last time God worked on my spirit, I saw a preacher whose feet never touched the floor and today, miles away from home stood a preacher with golden shoes on that Clay said was a dark color. I saw a color that reminded me of a beautiful sunset. I looked around to get an indication of some of those sophisticated women. I know at least one of them saw that those shoes didn't match that suit. Or was God trying to tell me something else?

"Stand firm saints against the forces of the devil. Job stood his ground. The devil tore him up, tore him out, and left him to curse God and die. Job was even encouraged by those whose love he cherished the most. His wife told him, after several days of pain, to curse God and die.

"What did you ever do for God that would cause Him to treat you like a two-bit criminal? I wish He would ask me what I think."

I could just see our ladies addressing God on behalf of their spouse. We'd be in worse shape.

"God took all He gave you. Why'd He give to you then if He knew He was going to take it all back? Who'd ever heard of an Indian giving God? Give it and then take it away. You're a lot better than me Job. I'll tell you want you ought to do. Tell God how you feel, let Him know He ain't right and you're sick anyway and you have nothing so then just give up your life and gone 'bout your business!" Job looked at his wife funny. And what do you think he said?"

The congregation was roaring with laughter and serious praise comments. The pastor had put us on a level we could understand. I could see myself telling God a few things. I would have probably done mine without the added encouragement of my spouse or loved ones. I would not have been like Job and taken the high road. Job was keeping it real. I would have kept it real but on my real terms. I refocused. The pastor had not spoken. I wanted to hear what Job told his wife. I already knew what he told her. I just wanted to hear it from Pastor Dames. He walked back to the front of the podium. Although I was still intrigued by his sermon, I was compelled to look at his shoes again. I saw the golden shoes glitter even in the dimness of the church. I gasped and tried not to alarm Clay who was ignoring my surprise any way. I wanted to know why his shoes were gold and no one else saw them but me. I hurried back to the sermon as to not miss the good points of surviving a satanic attack. I was being readily attacked but not by Satan. I took one last stare at the gold shoes and returned to the sermon.

"What do you think Job told his wife? What would you have said is the real question?" The pastor laughed at his own humor. Most of the congregation joined him in his short laughter.

"Job told his wife she was crazy and that God wasn't the one calling the shots on this one. *Like crazy He ain't to blame,* his wife responded. *He's the one flipping the script.* Job refused to believe God had a hand in this madness. This went on for some days. Job never gave up. He stood firm with his belt of truth and his breastplate of righteousness. Still, he stood firm."

The pastor's voice went to a clam whisper. He moved from the podium to the back and then came back in front of it. He moved across the floor near the place where all of his supporting deacons sat. He faced them as if speaking directly to them he said, "My brethren, you must identify your enemy. Your enemy is not flesh and blood; it's the spirits of evil forces. Job knew that there was no enemy on earth causing him such hardship. He blamed himself and his thoughtless actions for his tragic moments. He did not ever blame God. He encouraged his family to feel the same way by not entertaining comments like his wife's. When we entertain others comments on our situation, we are taking off the whole armor of God. In order saints to survive a satanic attack you must know that man ain't the enemy. Man has never been you enemy." He was still whispering.

I looked at his shoes. They were still fiery golden. I would ask one of the ladies after church. She surely saw those bright sun rising colored shoes with that metal gray suit. The pastor made a hand gesture. The pastor's aide snapped to him with a fresh cloth and a robe. I admired her precision. I know she knew that the pastor wore those brightly colored shoes. Somebody knew, well not Clay. He said he didn't see them and that I needed my eyes checked. I saw them!

After a few sporadic pauses, he returned to the podium. The shine from the shoes disappeared behind the podium. As he wiped his face with the fresh cloth, he repeated to the congregation in a soft pleading voice.

"You can survive a satanic attack. Just be able to identify your enemy. That's easy because you'll have the same enemy all the time. To reassure you turn with me to St. John 8:44."

Bible pages shuffled slowly. The saints were quiet.

"If you have it, say amen."

The "amens" rang in soft whispers throughout the church. The pastor wiped his face once more before he spoke.

He took a breath and began softly, "You are of your father the devil and anything he says you'll do. He was a murder from the beginning and he was never concerned about the truth because there's no truth in him. When he is lying, it's all him and no others. He is the creator of all lies. Now because I'm telling you the truth, you don't believe me." But you have to believe me saints. The devil is the ringleader of your attacks. If you want to be angry at something or someone, blame the devil. Now turn back with me to Ephesians 6:11."

Bible pages flipped more vigorously this time. I was excited to know that I didn't have to stress when the devil came upon me. I turned to the scripture and waited. I made ready my pen and notebook.

"Put on the full armor of God so that you can survive a satanic attack. You are not fighting against people but rather an evil spirit. The devil attacking you is not an earthly battle therefore nothing on earth can overcome it. The spiritual armor of God can protect you. Therefore, my brethren put on the full armor so that one day you can stand against the evil and then afterwards still stand. After all you have done, you can still stand. When times get hard, keep standing knowing that God will take care of you. God will always be there when you are going through a satanic attack. Amen and God bless you." His voice never rose and the pastor's aide gracefully removed the pastor's suit jacket and replaced it with a long black and gold robe. He stepped away from the pull pit. The gold on his robe matched his golden shoes. I gasped but said nothing.

"I have armor to wear. I need to make sure I get a set for each of my children and one for my husband. I just will never find anyone who'll love me like Jesus. I'm going to survive. I am," I said happily. "We are."

I also wanted to know the significance of the golden shoes. The shoes were just like the boat in the desert, no need for them and it looked out of place.

Chapter Two

WE'RE GOING TO MAKE IT BECAUSE OF JESUS

I was starting my twenty eighth day at Ft. Benning, Georgia. I woke up on the hot Sunday morning knowing I'd attend church. I tried to motivate myself to go and be happy about being there. I missed my family and I missed my own church. It was eight o'clock. The Dining Facility would be closing in thirty minutes. I quickly showered, dressed, grabbed my cellular phone and headed out of the barracks. The three static rings felt like an eternity. I forced myself to speak pleasantly to whomever answered.

"Hello."

I'm sure the Motivator knew it was me. At home it was six o'clock in the morning on a Sunday. He knew. I smiled because I was so happy to hear his voice.

"Hi Baby," I was sure to speak softly and slowly. I walked toward the Dining Facility (DFAC) listening attentively to the Motivator's excited voice. I felt a spark of relief. The tone of his voice let me know that all was well at home. Hectic for sure. Chaotic of course, but everything was all in good order. I had to hurry. Clay would be here to pick me up shortly. I slipped into the DFAC and had a big breakfast.

The transportation van went by. I didn't see the driver. I sat outside on the bench. I redialed my home number. The Motivator answered on the second ring.

"Hello," he said in a soft voice.

"Hey Baby. I called back to listen to you some more." I silenced and waited for him to say more.

"Oh, that's good. I'll be getting up here in a minute to get ready for church. I was really busy last night. The boys had a basketball game and Earl had to leave early for school on Friday morning because his class went on a trip. And the girls are doing fine."

"Did he have fun?"

"Yeah, he had fun. He couldn't stop talking about it."

I smiled into the receiver. The Motivator was obviously motivated to tell me about the week's events. The white van pulled up to the curb.

"Hello Ma'am," said Clay. He gladly showed a set of pearly white teeth.

"Hello Sergeant," I replied. "Where are you going off to this Sunday morning?" I didn't ask the Motivator to hold on while I talked with the soldier. I wanted to ask him if I he was going to church. Ironically, he was on his way. He told me he'd be back and pick me up at 10:30.

"I'll be there. I'll stand in front of building 2836," I was sure not to yell across the walkway.

"I'll be there," responded Clay.

The Motivator talked about a few more issues and things then we kissed into the phone terminating the call. At 10:30, Clay pulled up in front of the tall fence. I was dressed and ready for Sunday morning service. I tried to remember the last sermon I heard before I was mobilized to Georgia.

Resurrection Sunday. My report date was April 22, 2003. The commander wanted everyone to spend time with their family. I appreciated the commander's attention to detail: family support.

I stepped into New Jerusalem knowing I had a lot of questions needing answers. Nonetheless, I was happy to see my church family. As usual the choir sang two uplifting songs. I was moved by each of them. God still loves me I thought with a tearful heart. I was glad to understand that God really loves me. I was seeking relief of mind. I wanted God to remember to watch over me and watch over my family. The Middle Eastern countries would be our parting point. That was where I was scheduled to deploy. I stopped daydreaming to watch the pastor standing still in the pulpit.

    This pastor wasn't Pastor Leonard. He and his family had moved to Michigan in the spring. He was called to pastor a new flock. Though my spirit missed him dearly, I listened closely to Pastor P. King. I envisioned Pastor Leonard's angelic voice. He was calmly preaching to his new congregation. I watched Pastor P. King's six feet tall frame fill the height of the ceiling in the pulpit area. He was extremely well dressed. He wore a navy-blue two-piece suit. His shirt was a lighter shade of blue. He was not as handsome and angelic looking as Pastor Leonard. He was however, very educated and confident. I was sure his soul was right. Those traits at the time were very important to me. He began to speak. His voice was heavy and sounded as though he was giving a seminar at a prestigious institution. Educated and a serious tone with a mixture of over-confidence. I thought, fantastic, as I shivered in my seat.

"What was the text, pastor?" The lady sitting next to me blurted out silently.

"I'd like to know it too," I whispered back in her direction.

"Saints," cried out the heavy voice. The sound seemed to have shaken the church and then there was an awkward pause. "There are stories in the Bible that have been told over and over and over. Today you'll hear about one of those stories glorifying a hero. Resurrection Sunday: The story of Jesus rising from the dead. Saints, please stand for the word of God."

Members stood all over the church.

"Now go to Matthew 28:1."

I didn't. Instead, I slowly read the scriptures in a whisper. Pastor P. King read heartily aloud.

"…Do not be afraid…He is not here…go quickly and tell His disciples…They went out with fear and great joy."

Pastor P. King's voice rang out over the pulpit with smooth projection and confidence. "My text title is *Jesus is a Living Legend*."

At that moment I prayed asking God to please bless my family and me. I wasn't in the place where I wanted or really needed to be so I thought. I also really wanted to let the Word work for me.

"Please bless my entire family. I really need Your love and really need You." I wasn't sure if I was speaking too loudly. The lady sitting next to me turned her head. She smiled in my face and asked if I got the text title. I nodded and returned the warm smile. It was truly a good day and maybe I was where I was supposed to be in Christ and yes, the word was definitely working. The pastor directed us to take our seat. I whispered "amen" and kept reading. April 20, 2003, Resurrection Sunday. Jesus is a Living Legend for sure and I was on my way to Fort Benning, Georgia and then to the Middle East. I asked myself, *"would I still be where I needed to be and could I still let the Word work for me?"*

The white van pulled into the parking lot of Macedonia Non-denominational Church. I wondered why Clay took us to a different church that was a little closer to the base. I was curious to see the makeup of the congregation. I had just gotten use to Pastor P. King and I missed my New Jerusalem church family. I enjoyed watching the happy faces hug other happy faces. I just needed to hear a word from God, from a man of God. I got out of the van and headed into the church. Since we were a little early, I was able to pick a comfortable seat in the back. An usher came by my seat to have me fill out a visitor's badge. I politely refused. I felt or should've felt like a member. I didn't feel like a real member but I was excited to be there. Later I thought that it would've been a good idea to fill out the visitor's badge. I counted the pews. Not sure why, but I did.

The Praise Team, Choir, and Dance Team did an excellent job of witnessing to the congregation. Simply divine I silently shouted. I looked about the pulpit to see if I could "pick out" the pastor. There were no apparent signs or features indicating a "pastor". Each minister seated in the pulpit wore a simple black suit. None of them sparkled like Pastor L. Adames. I just had to wait to see which one would rightly divide the Word of Truth. I couldn't see their feet so I had to wait, still. I did just that, waited. I relaxed to listen to the choir's last selection. Splendid. The waiting door was opened.

"Do you have adversities in your life? Of course, you do. We all do!"

I watched the preacher move to the front of the pulpit as he spoke. His voice wasn't deep tenor or high soprano. It was more alto and reassuring. I relaxed a bit more and prepared to take in a Word from the Lord. I felt out of place because my small maroon Bible was back at the barracks. I pulled out the blue Bible from the book holder on the back of the pew in front of me.

"Please saints stand for the Word if you can..." I stood on order. I surprised myself. I didn't want to be blatantly disobedient in the visiting church. I also didn't want to be in a visiting church checking shoes.

"Please go with me to Ephesians chapter six and we'll begin at verse eleven."

I tried to remember if I got his name or if he'd even mentioned it. I wanted to write it down in my notes. I picked up the church bulletin. On the back was a list of the church staff. Pastor Scott Young Jr. was the pastor of Macedonia Non-Denominational Church. I wrote it in my journal. Nice name. I raised my head to watch Pastor Young's head point toward the podium. Before reading the assigned scripture, he raised his head. He must have memorized the verses because he spoke rather than read from his Bible.

"Put on the whole armor of God that ye may be able to stand..."

Regardless of how familiar, I needed to hear the rest, but my past got the better of me. The whole armor of God. We were training to support and fight a war. Are we really able to make it because of Jesus? Am I really where I'm supposed to be? I wanted to see the shoes. I didn't even know the significance of them, still I was anxious to see. The verses came to me in bits. Somewhere the pastor would say and when there's nothing else, stand. That was interpreted as stand and let the Word of God work for you. Even if you felt out of place or the blessing you were getting didn't fit, somewhere they would all come in handy. Sand, desert, and a great big boat. Who would believe we'd need it one day?

Chapter Three

LET THE WORD WORK FOR YOU

"…having your loins girt about with truth…" I listened as the pastor half spoke and half read the scriptures from his Bible. I listened, followed along in the borrowed Bible, and thought as I stood obediently for the Word of God. I thought about me just a short time before arriving at Ft. Benning.

"Mrs. Scottsville you have an important call on line two. Can you take it?" The secretary's voice was crisp. I adored her professionalism and tact. Knowing my response wouldn't sound nearly as professional and crisp. I cleared my voice and replied "yes", as I walked across the hall to take the call. I was certain it was private.

The voice on the other end was immediate. "They got you Captain Scottsville. They got you and you should be receiving orders by Friday or Saturday."

It was Wednesday. I immediately thought about my family getting by without me. Then I thought about confronting a real enemy. The whole armor would be needed.

The pastor stood silent. I didn't know what I missed. I decided to pay a little more attention.

"We all have an enemy. Everyday the devil is attacking somebody's life. The devil works full time to make your life miserable. The devil is your only enemy. You know when you go to work, the policy states that you get a fifteen-minute break or twenty-minute break for every four hours worked. Well, the devil doesn't take that kind of time." Pastor Young Jr. paused.

I listened to the response from the congregation. I smiled with comfort.

"He has nothing else to do! The devil," the pastor continued, "isn't going to say, I need a break, I just got off work, or I'll bother you tomorrow. Hold on a bit. He definitely isn't going to say it's been a hard day I'm going to take a nap! It's not going to happen." The pastor paused and made a face. I could hear the chuckling of the saints sitting behind me. He added, "It ain't that kind of party people!"

I laughed under my breath. I hadn't thought about the devil's job to that extent. I was aware that he does bad things but I hadn't realized that he did it all day, everyday, all the time.

"But saints, amen, you already got a way out." The pastor's voice suddenly began to roar with excitement. "You have got a way out," he repeated for emphasis.

I got excited right along with the message. There's a way out? That's terrific.

The scriptures were taken from Ephesians 6:11-17. A sermon I thought I'd heard before, I felt like I needed to hear it again. I read the verses as the pastor spoke to the congregation. I knew from reading that I'd heard it somewhere before and I'd learn something from it. I listened to it again I'd learn more. I tried to listen and read the scriptures...for we wrestle not against flesh and blood but…against spiritual wickedness in high places…take the shield…take the helmet…and the sword. The verses stung my soul for the second time. I learned early in life that each time a Word from God is presented a new meaning is gained or a further appreciation of truth is rewarded. Though the sermon felt familiar, the lesson would be an added value to my spiritual growth.

"I've often heard of people fighting the devil or the devil doing something to them. It was interesting to hear about the protection one could use to ward off the devil. It was a relief to know that there are ways to survive an attack from the devil. There were ways still to survive and move on with a righteous outlook on life. *"How to Keep the Devil Unemployed"*. You're going to survive. You're going to be able to lay off the devil and keep him out of work."

Pastor Young Jr. looked about the congregation as if asking for approval, agreement. The members were wrapped into his next sentence. I was wrapped but I also noticed the look on his face. Though the victory is yours, let's arm ourselves just the same. Pastor Young Jr. stepped away from the pulpit. I could hear myself breathing. I was anticipating an excellent message and anxious to know what to do to fire the devil. I wondered for a moment if I should be afraid. I wasn't. I just wanted to know what I could do to protect myself.

Momentarily the preacher stepped from the pulpit. I snapped by eyes to his shoes. They were fiery golden and it took all I had not to scream out in excitement and fear. The golden shoes did absolutely nothing for the pressed two-piece suit. I couldn't see the suit color but I was sure it didn't match the gold shoes.

"Fighting a satanic attack isn't an earthly battle. Although the devil is bothering you, God promises to fight for you."

God was fighting and I was taking my mind back to the way things were once upon a time…

I'm sure my brother was tired of running from Reno and Donel. Everyday after school (this was his third-grade year) Reno and Donel chased my brother half way home. We weren't even supposed to go home. We were to meet my oldest sister (who is affectionately referred to as the Coordinator in her adult years). I think I was equally tired. This particular Thursday Sardis was running. We couldn't leave him but I couldn't help him. I couldn't fight those boys. We needed some satanic survival protection right then. "Saints, we don't have to fight."

My thoughts returned to Pastor Young Jr. I smile as I listened because my brother is now thirty years old and we all survived those boys to include Reno and Donel. For many years of our young lives, we were attacked by Satan. And only today for this sermon did I realize that we had actually survived.

"Saints now that we understand that we don't have to fight, let me tell you what you need to do."

I was glad to know I hadn't missed perhaps the important part of the sermon.

"Know who the enemy is. Know whom to direct to God. As it states in the verse put on the whole armor of God so that…So that you are ready to give that devil's energy to God before throwing the first punch or any punch for that matter."

I sat, smiling and writing. It had been years since we fought as children. It had been even more years we had fought within our families as adults.

"Coriander, I'm tired of running from those boys everyday. What can we do?"

Sardis was a little guy but he was my brother. I felt like he was all my responsibility. We didn't have much at all but we did have each other. I didn't know what else to tell him.

"Pray."

"Pray for what Coriander?"

I watched his small chest going up and down from all that running. I laughed to myself because we were fast and we were good at it. Before I could answer Sardis had his own answer.

"I could pray for some muscles and then I could just beat them up. Reno and Donel and anyone who messes with me and of course you too. I could walk home or I could meet Bunny without problems and on time for a change."

Sardis didn't want to cry. I was hoping he didn't. He was almost twelve and I wanted for him to be strong and confident. But being strong and confident at age twelve didn't help us much in the present situation. Talking about a boat in the desert!

"I'll help you pray for some muscles Sardis. I'll help you pray to be strong so that you can protect all of your sisters." I wasn't sure at the time if that was a good idea. The Bible does tell us to seek and we shall find and knock and the door shall be open and ask and it shall be given. It also tells us that all things work together for good for those who believe him. I just had to get a handle on the believing part.

I tried not to cry as well. I was no bigger than my brother but we both had big hearts and that was important. I was familiar with Job's story but I knew nothing of the devil and his work. Muscle is what we both needed.

"After next week when I get my muscles from God, I won't have to run any more. Coriander if someone bothers you or the rest of you all, tell me and I'll take care of them right away with my new muscles." Sardis was sure that God was going to give him muscles next week. I cried inside because I wasn't sure if God could do all that so quickly.

The next week we still waited for Sardis because Reno and Donel did their thing and Sardis had to run.

"I take it you're not going to tell Momma or Daddy. I watched Ellery and Gramesheas walk a few feet ahead of us. I checked Sardis for any bruises. None. Relief set in because we really couldn't tell our parents. Aside from telling our parents, Sardis was so sure he'd get muscles to fight instead of run. Sardis was such a small boy. He really could've used those muscles. Where was our armor? If I had some, I'd have helped him. Ellery and Gramesheas hadn't chosen to fight as a way of defense yet. At the time, that was probably good. Nonetheless we walked fast to meet up with Bunny, which I thought was a bigger battle than Reno and Donel. Bring on the armor!

Know your enemy. Know that the devil never stops bothering you and remember that the battle isn't for you to fight because the Lord will fight it for you. I was happy to know that I don't have to run away from my attacker. I'm not mad at God about my brother. Three years ago, I couldn't tell you that. Three years ago, I would've been upset and having a face to face with God. I have grown so much and now I know that God truly loves me. I know that man and woman have made a mess of our beautiful country. America was a gift to us from God and we are steadily destroying her. I just didn't know at the time that we could have simply asked God to do the fighting. It would've really helped.

Stand firm against the satanic attacks for God will fight for you. *That* was our muscles.

A beautiful Sunday morning and I was extremely happy to be alive. I thought about the preacher in Georgia. It had been 8 months and three states later. I was excited that God had given me another chance to be among the living and to continue caring for my family. Yes, it was a very beautiful Sunday morning. The Army didn't need our chemical expertise for the war. I was sad in a way to get sent home and half of me was relieved because we, my family, just wasn't ready. Yes, it was a very beautiful Sunday morning.

I watched the pastor enter the sanctuary. He wore a long black robe. A gold cross set on each shoulder. The word pastor was written on each arm. Divine is the word that came to mind. My heart was filled with joy and my soul rejoiced. He walked past the pew in a way that told me he had an important Word from the Lord. He sang a song telling the congregation that God has a blessing with each of our names on it. I clapped and sang along. Not only did I have protection from the devil but I also have a blessing with my name on it.

"Turn with me if you please to my favorite book of the Bible. St. John 20:27…Be not faithless, but believing. Because thou hast seen me, thou hast believed, blessed are they that have not seen and yet have believed."

I read the scripture after the preacher's reading, I quickly read a few others to get a better understanding.

"As you take your seats, keep in mind that you got to believe." The seats crunched while Bible pages rustled. Believe even if you haven't seen. Believe and still believe. I wrote the scripture in my planner. Believing and not seeing is difficult.

I knew first hand that not seeing was more difficult. I'd only been home for three months and...

Time seemed to move too fast. I had about four days to report to the duty station. I wasn't nervous, afraid, excited, or curious. I really had no real feelings and I liked it like that. Several relatives and friends continuously reminded me that they'd pray for me. I thanked them. I intended to pray a very simple prayer. I was to the point where I'd say, "Whatever Lord, Amen." I was afraid to ask for anything specific because several families lost loved ones and I felt like there would be more loss. I wanted to serve the country and I wanted to care for my family. God is with me. I just couldn't see Him. As the days passed, I tried to put my heart and mind somewhere. But where? I am told God is with you but I didn't see Him. I never thought about seeing God because I'd grown accustomed to knowing He was caring for me. I was preparing to go to war and doubt consumed me. For years I'd celebrated blessing after blessing and hadn't thought much of them. Now standing in the moment of truth, I was consumed with doubt. Ready or not. The pastor said it all, "You Got to Believe".

I woke up this morning happy. The Motivator thanked God for everything. We showered, dressed, ate, and left. I was last to leave the house. Unfortunately, I was blocked in so I walked to the Motivator's church. The walk was short and refreshing. I stuck my head in the door and looked to the right. I didn't see the Motivator or any of the children. Finally, I recognized the Motivator's suit color. I walked toward the front of the church. I've never been comfortable sitting close to the front at any church. Not sure why, just didn't. The youth choir was singing. I squeezed in between the Motivator and my oldest son. I looked at him and winked. He smiled and winked back.

This would be my last Sunday with my family for at least a year. That would be a long time for all of us. A very long time.

The week seemed to pass by quickly. Every morning I checked and rechecked my bags. Every evening I rushed home to spend quality time with my family. It wasn't like we didn't do that already it was just that it would be a while before it happened again. The Motivator did nothing out of routine. He did nothing special for me or for the family. That was fine with me. Routine and we stuck to it. His co-workers asked why he hadn't taken off work. He told them about the relationship we established several years ago. We put forth much effort to withstand change. Change in a sense that I was ordered to leave my home for a year. The week prior to my departure was filled with mixed emotions. I explained to my younger children that I had to go work for the Army. I would be back shortly after my son Davel turned thirteen. My middle son Earl quickly calculated the time on the calendar. My girls, what about my girls?

"Mommy, that's a long time!"

Although he showed no apparent signs of excitement or disappointment, the words pierced my heart just the same. I didn't want to cry and now really wasn't a good time to cry. I sat back on the couch looking around the family room. All of a sudden it appeared smaller than usual. I picked at my blue dress. I just remembered I hadn't responded to the time factor.

"Yes, sweetie it is a good chunk of time. But I need for you to help Dad."

"Why does Dad need help?" Earl's face still showed no expression to indicate how he felt. My heart tightened. I already missed his conversation and I hadn't even left yet.

"I won't be here to help him put away the laundry, pick up you guys from school, cook, clean the house-"

"Take us to Family Video," Earl added.

Every Thursday we would go to Family Video and rent movies so long as everyone was doing well in school. Recently a Family Video opened closer to our house so we would walk to the video place. We would rent games and movies and have a game and movie marathon night and weekend. It was so much fun. I had no clue how to play the games and I always liked to rent horror movies.

"Right Earl. I won't be able to take you to Family Video so you'll have to remind Dad and help him pick good movies and games. I'm sure one of your sisters will help too." Earl sat staring aimlessly. It was his usual expression.

"Church?" I couldn't tell if he was asking a question or making a statement.

"What about church, Earl?"

I glanced over to him. Just then Elmon ran past. I didn't even tell him to stop running in the house. I saw that he had already changed his clothes. Earl and I sat on the couch still wearing our Sunday best. We looked like we were ready to go back to church.

"Yes Mommy, are you going to go to church while you're gone?" Earl looked right at me. He was so cute and handsome that I reached to hug him. He returned a warm, sincere hug. Although he still wore no expression, I knew he was sincere. He's always good at being sincere and loving.

"Let's make a deal. If you keep up with your school work and pray for me every day, then I'll stay safe and be back before you're ten years old."

Earl stared blankly into my face. I glanced down to see his crisp white shirt; Tasmania devil tie covered with his coal black suit jacket from Sears in Bloomington. The ride was long and well worth the trip. I took his hands that were partially covered by the new jacket.

"So, is it a deal?"

"Is what a deal? How can I say yes if I don't know what it is?" The same blank, yet sincere stare pressed against my face.

"What do you think it means? Think about what I want you to do."

"Be good."

"What else?"

"Do good in school and pay attention to the teacher."

"And what will I do?"

"Be here for January 6. What about Dad's birthday? Are you going to be here for his birthday too?"

"If you do like I asked then yes I will."

The smile covered his blank, sincere stare. "That's great. Now I need to go change my church clothes Mommy."

I watched Earl slide off the couch. He trotted lightly to the stairs and paused as if thinking of more to say. Then he disappeared up the second floor. I sat alone on the couch perhaps with a blank stare too.

I wondered what I could do to get out of going. I was afraid to push the issue because I was too afraid to find out that I'd have to go later and maybe to somewhere worse. But what's worse than not being at home? No place. Regardless of where I'd be sent, I'd still be separated from my family. Let the Word work for you. I had to trust God on this one.

I knew I'd miss my family and both of those birthdays but I also knew we'd be fine.

The television spilled out color and sound. Both were meaningless. I glanced out the family room window. I knew it was close to dinnertime. I rose from the couch and headed upstairs to set out the evening meal. I didn't bother to adjust the volume on the television. Like our van, we had one of those televisions whose sound adjusted with the noise level of the room. I just let the volume work for me. I wondered if it could be that simple for trusting Christ to do what He needed for me.

I couldn't remember if I heard the Motivator coming in or not.

At the end of the week, I was gone from my home heading to Minnesota and then to Wisconsin. God was going to take care of my family. I was sure to take my armor with me because I knew I'd need it. I just didn't know exactly when and wanted to "stay ready".

I reminded myself to let the Word work for me.

Chapter Four

JESUS HAS SOMETHING TO TELL YOU: HE WANTS YOU TO LISTEN

I wanted the dinner to be special. I knew I wouldn't prepare or serve the next Sunday meal. I didn't cry. I opened my ears to hear all the background noises. I could hear the shouts from the PlayStation and the music from the Game Cube. I could hear the Motivator in the garage probably moving stuff to get his boat in it. I told myself not to worry. I'd have a chance to hear it all again. I'd just come in from church. While at church, I heard plenty of background noises: babies crying, adults talking in whispers, and teenagers passing notes. I should've listened for Jesus. What if He had something to tell me? I wiped my hands on the sides of my dress. I couldn't have been nervous but maybe I was. I walked about the house wondering about the day's events. Jesus has something to tell me and He wants me to hear it. I wondered if I'd be able to hear Him like I could hear the background noises.

The day was really hot. The walk from my work tent to the chapel seemed longer today. It could've been because I wore all of my gear due to last night's change in protection posture. I sat in the chapel. The military refers to its churches as chapels. I'm going to the chapel for service as opposed to saying I'm going to church. Funny but I was able to make a quick transition in terminology. The wooden chairs gave me an old fashion feeling. I counted the rows. It was a lot more than ten of them and there were no pews. There was no way I could spread my planner and Bible across the seat as I'd done so many times in the United States. At the moment I didn't miss home. I was moved by the day's events and wanted to learn some of the new songs.

Later in the week I decided to join the choir. As a choir member, I was required to sit up front. I'd never sat that close to the front of a church or a chapel. I was, however, anxious to see if the Army preacher had on golden boots. Our boots were sandy brown like the color of the desert. I was happy today to be in the back but I knew I'd have to move closer once I became an official choir member. I leaned over to see the Army preacher's boots. When he came into full view, I closed my eyes. I wasn't ready for this part yet. I was too far away from home. I kept my eyes closed for a while. I'm sure my fellow soldiers thought me praying or sleep. If they knew, what would they do or say? I wasn't ready to answer questions about my sanity in conjunction with my spirituality. I didn't understand the reason for the golden shoes, not yet. I'd have to sit closer next Sunday and that was my focus.

I guess closer to the front would help me to hear much better. I'd see. I was required to sit on the second set of chairs. A big move for me. I braced myself to get ready for the "big move". Opened ears and up close and personal with Christ listening to a preacher with golden desert boots on his feet. Maybe.

Jesus definitely had something to tell me and I'd better get ready to listen.

I pressed my hands on my uniform. The wrinkles reappeared. I wasn't sharp looking but I was happy. Being a choir member also required me to come early and have prayer. I thought I could hear Christ since it would only be a few of us present. I wanted to know my real purpose for being overseas. I wanted to know the reason for the gold shoes and boots maybe and I didn't want to just ask God directly. I was growing in Christ and I liked my progress. I wasn't ready to give up so easily. I guess I would just have to let the Word work for me. Normally I would've gone face to face with God demanding a direct answer. No work on my part. I'd be falling back into my old self and I didn't want that. The past three years worked wonders for me. I'd grown so much and was beginning to not only understand God's plan but to accept it as well. I still wanted to know why. Maybe not so soon and not just a direct answer from heaven.

"Mrs. Scottsville, I need to see you please. Can you come by tomorrow?"

I listened to the crisp voice on the answering machine. She didn't sound like there was a serious problem but I could tell in her voice that she wasn't pleased with whatever it was she needed to speak to me about. I listened to the entire message. I scratched the number on the first available paper and then checked the clock. The middle schools were still in session. I quickly dialed the number. A pleasant voice sang hello and asked if she could help me.

"Yes, I'd like to speak with Ms. Hightowers."

I played with the paper while I waited for her to locate Ms. Hightower. I could hear the secretary's heels getting closer. She picked up the receiver.

"She'll be right with you."

"Thank you," I responded hoping I was polite. I played with the scratch paper while I waited. I looked at the clock. The minute hand sounded at 3 o'clock. My children would be home in 15 minutes.

"This is Ms. Hightowers. Can I help you?" Her voice sounded like a clone of the voice on the answering machine message. I could still hear the rattle of the background noise.

"Yes ma'am. My name is Coriander Scottsville. I'm returning your call. I'm sorry I wasn't able to come but let's talk."

"I'm sorry it took so long Mrs. Scottsville. I'm concerned about Davel's grades."

I could hear the sincerity in her voice. "Davel's a really well-adjusted student. He's quiet, has excellent mannerism, and he does work hard. But right now, he's holding a C in Science and that's one of his stronger subjects. I understand that you work with him every afternoon. I just hope nothings being missed."

I waited for Ms. Hightowers to say more. I remembered the high-spirited brunette bouncing from the hallway to her homeroom.

"Yes, I understand. Please keep in touch and I'll do the same." I felt better after returning the receiver to its cradle. I thought about my entire family and my entire life up until the moment of returning a phone to its cradle. I had to leave my family for 445 days. I wondered if God would take care of us as simply and stress free as my phone call with Ms. Hightowers?

I looked at the clock. Davel would be home in ten minutes. I hustled from the bedroom to the kitchen. I checked the menu board to read: hamburgers and big French fries. The Motivator wanted short order dinner. I was certain all of them agreed on the menu before leaving for the day. I didn't recall seeing very many erasure marks on the menu board. I went into the garage to see if anyone had been proactive. There in the sink was ground beef. In the freezer were curly fries and six bags of super-sized precut frozen potatoes. Next to the sink was a grocery bag filled with raw white potatoes.

I reached for the bag and was startled by the opening of the garage door. Davel wore his birthday jeans. It was the third time this week. He had on a stale blue shirt with dingy white stripes on the sleeves. His shirt was large enough to fit me. I was on the verge of screaming when he stepped out of the glare of the winter sun. I didn't bother asking about a coat. I knew the answer.

"Hi Mommy."

"Hi Davel. How was your day?"

I watched his smile fade a bit perhaps from the tone of my voice. He shuffled from side to side. I cut right to the chase.

"Davel, be sure to turn in all of your work."

"Okay Mommy."

That was the end of the conversation. I knew he'd do as I requested. I had something to tell Davel that he already knew. He listened. He read my face, listened to the tone of my voice, and waited. Is listening for God that simple? God has something to tell you today and it's real good and He wants you to listen. I decided to modify it; it's real good for you and He wants you to listen.

I sat up straight in the hard chairs. The tent was hot again as it was last Sunday. I readied myself as the Sergeant pressed on the breast pockets of his uniform jacket. I strained to read the name on his name tag but he began introducing himself so I released the strain. God has something to tell me. Curtis Rendon. Am I ready to listen? I hope so. I stared at the full-mouthed, medium figure at the podium. He was apparently bubbling with joy. I was pulsing with sweat but smiled because he was so happy. It made me happy too. I wrote in my planner, Staff Sergeant C. Rendon. In the military first names weren't of much importance to me. Look at the nametag and remember the last name.

"I know this isn't like real church. I know the building isn't like some of your fancy Victorian cut furniture churches back in the U.S. This is a real church with real surroundings just not like your normal surroundings at home. Yet God is still in the blessing business, He's still in the midst, and He still wants to tell you something. Turn with me please to Proverbs 21."

The medium figure pressed on the breast pockets of his uniform while the pages turned. I wondered why the preachers always say turn with me to the scriptures and why soldiers press on the breast pockets of their uniform. Nonetheless I turned my Bible to the selected scripture. I felt nostalgic. I turned the pages more quickly to Proverbs 21. The medium figure hadn't mentioned a specific verse so I began from verse one. *The king's heart is in the hand of the Lord...He turns it whichever way he wants at his will. The way of man is forward and strange, but as for the pure, his work is right.* I didn't understand what the words were telling me. I continued to read.

Do what is right by the Lord for it is much better than sacrifice, I read in the verses. I always thought that serving the Lord was a sacrifice. I wasn't sure of the verses and what they meant. In my pondering I missed the verses Staff Sergeant Rendon announced. I continued to read from Proverbs 21.

The proud heart is a sin and the plans of the diligent are prosperous. Progress made by a tongue of untruth is deadly and the violent refuse to do what is right. When justice is done it brings smiles to faces.

I read on and on while the preacher spoke. I heard him say, "Proverbs 21:13, 21 and 30.

He that followeth after righteousness and mercy findeth love, righteousness and honor…There is no wisdom nor understanding nor counsel against the Lord.

"Jesus has something today and its real good and He wants you to listen."

I waited for the verse number but located it before the Army preacher continued. I was hearing but I didn't quite understand.

Follow a righteous path and find honor. There is no counsel against the Lord.

Maybe I couldn't hear the really good something or maybe I couldn't hear him. The generator howled in the background; the sandstorm moved to give a more deafening effect while the preacher made every effort to bring the Word to the congregation. If my name was called three times, I didn't hear it.

The tap on my left shoulder was the only thing that got my attention. I slowly turned to face the young soldier. Sergeant Presige. I commented on his name and congratulated him on his recent promotion. He whispered something in my ear about the commander. I nodded. Smiling after he'd delivered his message, he told me he called me three times and I didn't respond until he tapped my shoulder.

The medium sized Staff Sergeant Rendon clapped his hands and repeated his last sentence. "There is no counsel against the Lord."

I still didn't understand. Nonetheless I still closed my eyes or reverted elsewhere when the preacher moved from behind the podium. Yes, there was something I needed to know about golden shoes and maybe golden boots but not this Sunday.

My heart leaped as I returned my attention back to the Army preacher.

"You, as the Christian, have to possess the ability to get rid of the background noise."

That was my cue. I always listened for the background noises. I thought I was doing something extra for myself by being able to listen and hear the background noises. I guess I was wrong. I was basically interfering with what God was trying to tell me. I was listening to the background noises instead of listening for the real message. I snapped back into the Sunday sermon.

"Don't be like the Sunday Christian. Don't be in a noise zone during the week. You can't hear God. We have the Christian who is all ears on Sunday and deaf mute when the benediction is given. God wants to talk to you in the quiet of the day. The times when you are at home preparing for the night. The times when you are the only one in the office for the day. The times when you are on the battlefield waiting for the enemy. That's when God wants you to hear Him."

The Army preacher went on and on about how we need to be ready to hear a Word from the Lord. He even told us that a church gathering was probably the last place God would really speak to us. I guess because of the background noise. I was sure to listen more attentively and block out the background noise.

Immediately after the sermon, I headed back to the Control Point tent to see what the commander wanted. I made a note to walk through the loud area quickly. It was a dangerous spot. I concluded that I probably missed all of the calls while going between the generators. I'd also missed them during a severe sandstorm. If I were about to be attacked, no one would hear me because the generators were so loud and I'd be told that I purposely put myself in a dangerous position. Jesus has something to tell you and it's good and He wants you to listen. Get out of the noise so you can hear Christ. I pulled the door of the Control Point tent.

The weak air from the air conditioner pulled me into the tent. I looked around the tent. I didn't see the commander. I wandered immediately if I had heard Sergeant Prestige correctly. I strained my memory. I was blocked by the faint sound of the generators. I missed that message or was it one? I wasn't sure if I'd actually missed the message because I was blocked in by noise, uncontrollable noise or I just didn't hear. That started to bother me.

"The Lord has a message for you to hear," said Staff Sergeant Rendon.

I think I finally understood the Biblical message Proverbs 21:13.

"Whosoever stoppeth his ears at the cry of the poor..."

I wasn't plugging my ears. I really didn't hear the Sergeant calling me. I then realized I couldn't remember the entire message he'd whispered in my ear. Maybe I was in the wrong area trying to enforce situational awareness. Had I sat on the other side of the chapel, I would've heard my name the first time. My ears were opened but I wasn't in a position to receive the message therefore here I was standing in the Control Point tent waiting to see the commander.

God had something to tell me. It was really good and I needed to listen.

What was it?

The brief on Anti-terrorism told us what the enemy might do in certain situations. I came back to the attention of Sergeant First Class Dundley. She was telling us that the enemy tries to upset us or throw us off track. The enemy government uses propaganda to persuade the enemy's populace into believing that all Americans are bad. The media has something to tell the public and they'd like for them to listen. Unfortunately, they do. She said that the enemy understands Americans to be impatient and almost always in a rush. She also stated that the enemy knows that we trust no one, not even our own at times. I'm glad I heard that portion of the brief. In other words, the enemy will tell us what he/she will do. Are we listening? Something needs to be told and I need to listen.

It was God's turn to tell me. What was it?

Chapter Five

WHAT IT MEANS TO REALLY KNOW GOD

"God is really good to all of us here. I've been here in the desert for about a month now. It's hot, it's sandy, it's miserable. But God is still really good to us."

I sat on the hard chair and was sure to listen closely. I calculated my own time in theater, which amounted to about seven months total to include a few weeks on the new camp. I agreed God was indeed good. I counted the pews.

"He is. I was reading in the Bible about how good He is to us and I'd like you to come with me today and see what's in His name."

I sat in the seventh pew about the third spot from the left. I thought about my experiences from the tenth pew. It seemed like a long time ago. I thought about my last conversation with God; Did God make a mess? No, He did not. God gave us charge over all the animals. All living was placed under our feet. We, man, caused the trauma of today.

God never intended for us to suffer. Man disobeyed God's commandments and took away the beauty of the world He created for us. Maybe I was making progress I wasn't sure but I felt like I'd come a long way from the tenth pew.

Did I really know God at this time in my life? Was I still fishing for solid ground? No. I had made progress. A lot of it. I was just still learning God and what's in His name. I placed my attention back on the brief. To my amazement the brief was over. I'd missed the important portions. I had no notes and would shamelessly ask someone for theirs. I reminded myself to be more aware in my efforts to multi-task.

"Sell all you have. Sell it all and give it to the poor. Church, we ask what does it mean to really know God? I want to tell you about the rich young ruler. As a matter of fact, let's take that as my text title "What's in a Name Rich Young Ruler?" It sounded as if the tile was made up on the spot rather than studied and formed over some days. Nonetheless, I pulled out my pen and wrote at the top of the page, "What's in a Name, Rich Young Ruler" followed by October 30, 2004. I'd been on my new camp for about three weeks. I was fitting in and making adjustments. I wrote Sergeant Xavier under the text title. Sergeant Xavier was a young preacher with obvious potential. I'm sure he wasn't old enough to be popular, but I could be wrong. I was also certain that this was probably his first sermon on base, perhaps the first one ever. He looked to be no more than twenty-five years old. I took in the cleanliness of his uniform and overall appearance. He definitely wore the young man of God look. He had a shiny bald head and bright eyes that seemed to dance when he spoke. What's in a Name Rich Young Ruler? I readied myself to hear about a popular name and a rich young ruler from a spiritually rich young preacher with just a name.

"What's in a name? Have you ever reacted to a name that is recognized by many? If Michael Jordan, Madonna, or Brad Pitt walked into this chapel right now we would have another war on our hands. If Halle Berry, Vivica Fox, and Brittany Spears followed behind them the church would empty out and I'd have to preach this sermon next Sunday!" The church swelled with laughter. I laughed too. Such a young preacher. The laughter simmered and the young soldier continued. "What's in a name? Those same stars don't even have to be here physically. I could just mention that they'll be in the PX parking lot tomorrow and folk will skip work to go see them. You know you would church."

More laughter circulated throughout the chapel. I giggled too.

"Now I guess you need proof that Jesus' name is popular too. I get that for you. I'm going to Mark 10:17-23. Come go with me." The Bible pages turned and members stood. I was pleased to see the older and middle-aged stand up for the Word of God coming from such a young preacher. I flipped to Mark. The sound of flipping pages stopped. The young Sergeant looked about the congregation and began reading.

"Verse 17 says there came one running and kneeled to him asking what shall I do, good one, to gain eternal life? Why call me good? There's only one good one, He is God. To gain eternal life you must keep the Good One's commandments and honor the parents. He responded Lord these things I have always done and continue to do. Then said Jesus *sell everything you have and give it to the poor and follow me.* The man thought about it and then with a frown asked, "Follow you? What do you have my Lord?" He paused and replied, "I have my name."

The young preacher stopped reading and looked out into the congregation. For the rich young ruler, what was in a name? The Lord only had His name to offer but the rich young ruler didn't understand. I wrote the points on my paper. The young Sergeant's eyes danced as he readied to speak. He continued with spirit and motivation.

"You make take your seat if you can. The Lord only had His name to offer the rich young ruler. He explained to him like this: In my name you shall have eternal life. In my name you shall be saved. In my name you will cast out evil and heal the sick and raise the dead. In my name you will move mountains and help the weak out of deep valleys. In my name you can walk on water and turn rocks into bread. In my name you can tell others of my good works and they will follow you to eternity. You can do these things. All in my name."

The church was in an uproar with praises. I wrote quickly to give me time to watch the young preacher move about the pulpit. His eyes danced even more for he was filled with praise.

"Praise God, preacher."

"You go ahead young one."

"In His name. That's right!"

The Sergeant continued. I was excited myself. I knew my name was not too popular. Scottsville is going to be at the United Center doing a book signing next month. I could hear someone saying, "who is he or she? I don't know her or him!" But Jesus will be in London next month healing the sick. The plane seats would fill up! I put my attention back on the sergeant.

"But saints, Jesus saw the heart of the man and said, "it is impossible for the rich to enter the kingdom of God! You are a young rich ruler and perhaps your name is valuable in these parts. Your name is recognized by your people because you are rich. Because you have earth power." But again saints, what's in a name if it can't give you eternal life? That's what

I'm trying to tell you this evening. The rich young ruler was asked to sale all he had for Jesus. That's heavenly power isn't? Someone says there's Sergeant Xavier and the response is and what you want me to do? But with Jesus, His name means something.

"The name of the Lord was meant something to Eli and young Samuel. Turn to I Samuel 3:1-10." The preacher waited as the pages flipped to I Samuel the third chapter. Hold that thought. It was too long of a pause. I went back in time.

The day was cold but beautiful. I waited outside the Army center watching for a blue trailblazer or a cherry red town and country. I pulled on the sweatshirt and readjusted my bags. I'd been gone since December 10, 2003. The government gave us a four-day pass. I took it as an incentive to keep us motivated for our future ordeal. I didn't want to use my time reassuring the Motivator that God loves us and reminding the children to behave. While waiting, a soldier walked up to me.

"Excuse me ma'am, I may have a problem." I recognized the voice before turning to face her. I could feel her discomfort. I wanted the situation be comfortable. The best information is given when the subordinate is comfortable. I paused so that she wouldn't know I was anxious to know the details of the problem. When I faced her, my silence indicated that she could begin when she was ready. I looked at her attentively. I had learned in my resiliency courses to be an active listener. I watched her struggle to tell me her problem. I knew to be patient and not rush into the details. So, I waited. Private Rudan's face was red with fear or anxiety. She stammered and her face grew redder as she overworked her confidence to tell me the problem.

"I have a problem ma'am and I was told you're the one who would take the time to help me." Appreciation filled me as I watched Private Rudan. She paused and I wanted to say something like, Okay I know. Now out with it will you, but I held my tongue. Instead, I nodded for her to continue. God has something to tell you and He needs for you to listen. Maybe God was going to tell Private Rudan to tell me something. But she has a problem I reminded myself. This isn't about me so listen! I was however honored that my *name* was associated with doing something good for a fellow soldier.

"It is..." Private Rudan said quickly and paused again. I didn't want my patience to run out. ran out. She evidently trusted me or trusted my name.

"It is?" I replied with my most authoritative professional tone. I knew to wait again for Private Rudan to catch her breath and explain. So, I waited a little longer this time. Private Rudan appeared a lot thinner in civilian clothes. Her faded blue jeans stopped well above the rim of her high-top gym shoes. Although it was December, the salty look on her shoes indicated much wear in the warm months. She wore a black and red hunting top that was heavy and the oversized shoulders layered on her extremely narrow back. Private Rudan was a small, respectable soldier. I was sure to brace myself for a lengthy conversation full of pauses and deep thoughts. I realized later that they were not pauses but aggressive attempts to control her severe stuttering.

"My POA is supposed to pick me up here. She has a cell phone and I don't know. I don't know how to direct her here. She left an hour ago. I was wondering what should I do? When does this center close?" Private Rudan's face was red perhaps from the strain of getting her words out and ensuring I understood her. I did. I was glad to have been patient. You just never know what people are going through or what they've been through to get where they are. That's why it's so important for them to tell "the right person". She had said *my name* was mentioned.

"You can use my cell phone," I replied with gratitude. I was glad to be of help. "I have free nights and weekends so talk as long as you want and make as many calls as you need." I waited for her to show expression that she understood then added, "What's a POA? I heard many acronyms but I hadn't heard this one."

"Power of Attorney." Private Rudan was forceful and staggering in her reply. I was sure to wait a bit before I spoke. I wanted to be sure she'd completed her thought. I wanted her to hear the instructions I needed to give to help her marry up with her contact people. The culture and awareness brief had been informative. I learned that in the Arabic nations Iraqi and Kuwaiti people (the good ones) are generally patient. Ironic, one Sunday the post chaplain touched on us being patient, I thought as I waited for the soldier to gather her own thoughts.

In the end, I waited for over five hours for Private Rudan's ride. I didn't mind the wait. I went over and over in my mind, why people are placed in front of us as such. I guess my patience would help me through my desert experience; I didn't know.

Nonetheless, there was too much about my deployment that I didn't know. My name was mentioned and that alone made me feel special. Needed. There were many things I still didn't quite understand. I had to trust in God and let the Word work for me. There'd be satanic attacks for sure. I wanted to have the whole armor of God near me.

I sat on the chair. Events shuffling through that had taken place prior to my being here. I remember redirecting my attention to Sergeant Xavier. "What's in a name, rich young ruler?"

I planned to become more aware of my time and the season I'm in as it relates to my trials and serving Christ. More aware of my life. A reason to stay tuned into everything. But what about the background noises? I had to first learn to discern the times and the seasons because sometimes it's just not my time to go through a situation. God gives us the victory and we pluck it up and ruin it. I didn't want to do that. Culture and awareness were as important in my individual life as it was for life overseas.

God knows me very well and I'm trying to get to know Him a lot better. Really get to know Him. I'd add that to my things to accomplish: really getting to know God and know what it means to know Him. What it means to speak His name and know the power in His name. How could I get that done? Then it occurred to me...

"Turn with me to Hebrews the eleventh chapter and we'll begin at the third verse but keep a finger on I Samuel 3:1-10." Sergeant Xavier paused blankly as the pages of many Bibles turned. I turned quickly to the said verse.

"By faith we understand. By faith we can understand what it really means to know God. God created the earth and the heavens for all of us. But many of us will never understand God's love. Some of us will never want to understand God's love and many of us will accept God's love and know what it means to be loved by such a great and divine Spirit."

The congregation suddenly grew silent. This had to be a dynamic message. My rich young ruler. My own thoughts consumed me.

The day was pleasant and warm. I can't recall the date but I remember the words. It must have been Sunday school because

I remember commenting on those who will never know God and they were destined not to know Him. That day I could have made a really huge deal about God not taking care of His own. I didn't. I was growing and learning more and more about God's plan. This Sunday I was learning about God's love and what it really means to know Him.

"There are some people in the world who are destined to be ignorant of the Word of God." The male member sat back in his seat with a pleased look on his face.

I was not pleased with that comment. I held my tongue for about two seconds.

"How could you say that? How can you say that there are people in this world who are destined not to gain eternal life?" I tried to keep a polite tone.

"I didn't say they wouldn't gain eternal life. I said they'd be ignorant to the Word of God."

"That's the same thing. You're saying that you believe that there are souls that won't ever know the gospel but it's not by their choice. How could you say that?" I wasn't sure if my tone changed asking the question. I did all I could to remain calm. I took a quick glance about the church. The group was small and I definitely wasn't in the mood to make a scene. Get a point across yes; nothing more.

"Remember the parable about the seed sower?" said the male member.

"Yes, I do," I replied hoping I sounded cooperative, not hostile.

"Well, the Word or receiving of the Word of God is similar to the parable about the seed sower. Mark 4:4 tells you about the seed sower and what happened to the Word of God." I didn't even look up. I snapped my pages to Mark the fourth chapter and began reading quickly from the beginning. When I got to the fourth verse, I understood the male member's point but didn't get his logic. I took a couple deep breaths.

"I guess according to this, some people won't ever get to know God."

"I think so."

I took the liberty of reading a few more verses. I came to verse twenty-six and read to the end of the chapter. The kingdom of God is like the sower placing seeds and wherever they fall, life goes on regardless. Whether the seeds are cared for or not, the seed sprouts and grows. Whether we hear the Word of God or not, the gospel is still preached and is available to those who want to hear and accept it. I was still lost.

The sermon.

"By faith, we can understand what it really means to know God. God created the earth and the heavens for us. But many of us will never understand God's love. Some of us will never want to understand God's love and many of us will accept God's love and know what it means to be loved by such a great and divine Spirit." Sergeant Xavier spoke softly. "Go to I Samuel."

I almost cried.

I added to my spiritual library that very day that we all are given the chance to know God. We just have to take it. We have to take the time to get to know the *power* in His name. Then I listened to the events of I Samuel the third chapter.

"The young child in I Samuel heard his name called. He ran to Eli to ask him what he wanted of him.

"Yes Eli. It is I, Samuel. What do you want of me? You called."

"Sorry son. I didn't call you. Go back to bed." Samuel went back to bed. Moments later he heard his name. Again, he jumped up and went straightway to Eli.

"Yes sir. You called me and here I am. What can I do for you?"

"I did not call you child. But this time when you hear your name again just say, Lord here I am. What do you want of me?"

"Samuel's name was important. Eli told Samuel that he was answering to the Lord. Samuel knew that the task would be important. What's in a name rich young ruler?"

What does it mean to really know Christ? I knew now. The name of Jesus is powerful. His name is the power source of our lives. At times we feel like we can't grasp the pieces of the perfect plan. I guess that isn't our job, our calling. What does it mean to really, I mean really truly, know the Lord? I left church with the task of getting to know Christ. Much better of course.

It was another Sunday evening. I watched the Colonel walk up to take her seat in the pulpit. I looked at her from the waist up. I still didn't understand why I was seeing bright gold shoes. I'm almost sure Sergeant Xavier wore gold boots. I vowed to place only close attention to the word of God, not do boot checks. I was here this evening to really get to know Christ. I didn't know how and I wasn't going to ask. I was only going to listen and absorb. The Colonel was dressed in a jet-black robe. She looked simply divine. I stared at her and was temporarily captivated by her appearance. Although she appeared to be deathly skinny, her confidence struck me as riddled with strength. The congregation was terribly quiet and that was usual and a bit frightening for me. A young female Sergeant was giving order to the service. She stood I believe about five feet nine inches. She was very athletic looking and seemed to be very much in love with the Lord. She waved her hands and praised Him silently. I read the movement of her lips as she repeated over and over "oh Jesus, oh Jesus". This was allowed to go on for almost three minutes. No one dared to tell her time was wasting. Not on the Lord's time. Not in His name. After a couple more minutes the Sergeant gained her composure and addressed the congregation. She told us her name was Staff Sergeant Postit. She let us know how very happy she was to be in the presence of God. I smiled and said to myself, "me too."

"I remember a few Sundays ago when Sergeant Xavier preached about the rich young ruler and the name of Jesus. I know that His name is powerful and there is no other name like His in all God's creation. Thank You Jesus." Staff Sergeant Postit spoke softly yet with great compassion for the Lord's sake. She let us know in her tone and posture that Jesus was a serious part of her life. I agreed and smiled at her bravery and commitment. She read the scripture for the day and called the choir to minister in song. The Praise Dance Team followed worshipping to the song "Praise is What I Do". The Sunday service was going well and I was enjoying myself. Today I was going to understand what it really means to know God. What is really in the name Jesus and the power it provides? I sat and listened to the Colonel rightly divide the word of truth and in the end, I was hoping to know Christ better. It was perhaps my time and season.

Chapter Six

DISCERNING THE TIMES AND SEASON

Launch out into the deep and let your net down for a catch. You've been in shallow waters. "Be sensitive and discerning in the season you're in. The state of your life isn't accidental but prophetical. We need to hear what the Holy Spirit is saying. Be sensitive to God's voice and actions."

There was a short pause. I opened my eyes. I think they were closed. The lady preacher stood in the middle of the pulpit inside the military chapel. A high-ranking field grade officer was rightly dividing the Word of truth. I'd never seen it done in all my years of military service. I was able to read her nametape: Colonel Groct. I dare not pronounce it aloud. I'd address her as ma'am and be done with it.

I smiled with joy of being present in the house of God thousands of miles away from home. The homely atmosphere made me feel just that: as if I were home. I pulled out my little palm Bible ready to hear the scripture. The Bible was so small I smiled at it and thought.

"Coriander, be prayerful and keep peace. God will take good care of you."

I watched my mom's lips move frantically. I knew she'd miss me but I also knew that her faith in God would relax her. God was my mom's best friend. He had a standing prayer to take care of my mom's children and husband and all of her grandchildren. I couldn't worry because God loved my mother with all of His heart and she reciprocated a mere fraction of His love to Him. Nonetheless it was a relief to know that God still loved my mom and she still loved Him. That meant more blessings in my corner. She knew what time and season she was in and I was about to learn. I relaxed at her touch to my face.

"And be sure to read your Bible all the time." She still looked like an angel.

"I don't want to take my good Bible because it might get taken. You know the one you gave me, that I paid for. I've read about the cultures and I'm afraid that customs may keep mine."

"I'll get you a smaller one. You need to have a Bible. Of all things you need a Bible." She smiled and her angel like qualities lifted my spirits.

"I know I'll need one. I need to stay abreast of the Word." I returned a smile.

"You also may want to witness to others about God's great works." I stuttered for a reply. Mom never really told me face to face about witnessing. She never really said "Coriander, you need to witness to people. You can do it. Nothing along those lines. She'd remind us to be thankful and prayerful but I don't recall ministering.

"I don't know how I could get that done where I'm going. I know it'll be important but how would I know if it's my calling?" I wasn't sure if was genuinely concerned about the culture or simply fishing for an excuse not to minister to others. I didn't want mom to be disappointed. Is ministering my calling? I had to discern the time and season for me. I wasn't ready to help others because I felt like I was still helpless. That's selfish, isn't it?

"Turn with me if you will to Ephesians 4:1. Take your time and find it because this here is important news for the Christian. While you search, I'll talk. I was thinking just the other day that everybody isn't called to a ministry. Everybody isn't called to present God's Word to His people. Some of you may *think* that you are the one but sometimes that isn't the case. Now if you're there say amen." The preacher walked about the pulpit as if checking to see if the members were following along. I read the first verse and then a few after it. The preacher roared out the first verse.

"I therefore beseech you that ye walk worthy of the vocation where with you are ordained. Let me repeat that for some of you. I therefore tell you to walk upright in the ministry that I've placed upon you." The congregation responded as the preacher continued to read. I followed along and a bit ahead and at one point returned to the first verse.

"As ye are called in one hope of calling. Everyone is given grace according to our measure of the gift of Christ. He gave some apostles, and some prophets and some evangelists and some teachers for the work of ministry. He gave some to some not all to everybody. That means saints that everybody is not called to present the Word of God. Only some and we will know if we are part of the some." The preacher pointed at no one in particular in the congregation as he spoke. I gazed at his extra-long finger extended from the pulpit. His gold watch dangled lifelessly on his boney wrist.

"I just want to use for a title today "The Call to Ministry." Along with that calling is a time in to report. Now don't get confused. The Spirit of Christ may have told you that you are one of the some for a calling. That doesn't mean you start barking out what you think what thus said the Lord over the pulpit! That means that what you think is God's today could mean twenty years for you. I know some of you are wondering well what about me? I have been a minister for years. You mean to tell me that I wasn't called. Are you saying I'm actually *not* ordained?"

I wrote the notes neatly. I was sure I'd have to return to them. "The Call to Ministry" Ephesians 4:1-10. I was feeling pretty good that maybe I wasn't called and terribly awful if I was called and didn't go. I put my attention back on the preacher.

"Saints let me share something with you. Those of you who are feeling a little conviction in your spirit are those of you who aren't sure. So, what I'm going to do is clear some things up for you and then you can have a better reading on where you are on the calling list. First, let me point out to you that some of you never had a calling." The congregation abruptly silenced. My mouth hung open along with about seventy-five others. I paid real close attention. Here I was thinking that...I don't even have the answer. Pay attention Coriander! You may be one of those who don't even know! I admitted I was. There praise phrases sounded weak as they bounced about the church. The congregation was on edge to hear the slender finger, boney-wrist, preacher tell us where we were probably wrong.

"I see that you all have gotten pretty quiet and that's fine. You need to know this anyway. Everybody isn't called forward or ordained to preach. And those who are called are not bought forward until God says you're ready. You are proven and prepared and called forward when you're ready. God doesn't call you before you're ready and those of you who just jump right in are those who weren't sent you just went!" The congregation loosened up just enough to get a little laughter out. A few praise phrases pinched through lips and I think the members wanted to get on to the next point.

"We cannot see the end results of God's choosing. Hence, we have to be proven and prepared and then called forward to minister to the people. Turn with me to Romans 1:1. It's not far from Ephesians so you should get there pretty quick. Say amen when you get there." The preacher waited. A few amens with a slight attitude engulfed the pulpit. I thought why get angry with the skinny looking preacher; the Bible tells us we have to be called. I'm not going that route I reminded myself and instead read verse one of Ephesians. *Paul a servant of Christ Jesus called to be an apostle to give out the gospel.*

"Paul was a servant of Jesus and he was called by Christ to preach the gospel. Now you're probably wondering, well how did he know? How do we know he just went and wasn't sent?" Another pause. "Saints, there are three ways of confirming your calling." I was thankful for the pause. I turned to a fresh sheet and wrote a number for each of the three points. I waited for the next words to spill out of the preacher's mouth. He extended his boney across the pulpit and spoke.

"There are three types of witnessing that goes on to prepare and prove your calling. The first kind is the intuitive witness. This witness can sense in his heart that the Lord is calling him to minister. The second is the confirming witness. This witness has the characteristics of the intuitive witness but she will wait before announcing her calling. The third witness is the demonstrated witness. This is the physical evidence that this particular individual had been called forward to present God's Word. So, find out which you are. Intuitive, confirming or demonstrative. If you cannot discern then it's probable not you, He's calling. It's probably not your season.

I hoped mom hadn't said too much. She didn't appear to have cared even if she had.

"Mom, I'll be sure and spread God's word as I see fit and the timing is right. I'd hate to force feed someone and I haven't been trained myself." I looked at her facial expression. It appeared that she was slightly disappointed in my statement. Well, that's how I felt. I just couldn't picture myself training up an adult in the way that he or she should go. I was about to make a come-back but mom spoke first.

"I didn't mean for you to do any self-ordaining. I just want you to remember to tell others how good God is to you. That's all God asks of us. Give a testimony. I said nothing of the sort in the way of lecturing, nagging, or preaching a sermon. Just remember to testify of God's goodness and good will come to you. Simply put, give God all the glory." Mom smiled her beautiful angelic smile. I can do that. Then suddenly, I immediately missed her. She was my heroine when it came to trusting Christ. I moved toward her arms in hopes of a hug. Although she didn't extend her arms, I could still feel her love surrounding me. We didn't do much hugging growing up but the genuine love was always there. Her words hugged me long and gently.

"Mom, I'll do that for us. I'll tell of my blessings and remember to testify every chance I get. I will mom. Thanks so much for being such a beautiful lady. That's so helpful." I stayed in proximity but there still was no hug. We talked more. I moved to leave when we heard the door. I knew it was my dad coming in from a long day of work.

Mom smiled once more and I returned one as big.

"Saints turn with me to Ephesians 3:1-9." The Colonel paused to allow time for us to find it. Colonel Groct was assigned as the base camp chaplain. She would bring the word this evening.

"To every thing there is a season…He hath made every thing beautiful and in his time." Colonel Groct belted out the verses with ease and confidence. She pressed both hands on her front pockets. As she walked about the pulpit, I heard the crisp sound of her fresh uniform. No robe today, I thought as if it made some difference.

"Christians are just like people who live in a fast-paced society. New York citizens are prime examples of the "now" word. We want to pray and hear an answer from God now! Instead of searching impatiently for an answer, find out what God wants you to do. Take the time to see how you should act. We simply need to wait on God."

I pulled out my little brown notebook. I wanted to take notes to tell when I returned home. As usual, I had plenty of paper, a good working pen, and I was waiting for the next words.

Shoes! I still wasn't quite ready to check for golden shoes. I pressed hard on my notebook and braced myself for the sermon of the century.

"There's a purpose, a season, a time for everything. God is overseeing the events of our lives. We just have to stay focused on God's works, although the devil wants us to focus on the calamities of the world." The Colonel strutted across the pulpit. The word was seamlessly echoing from the Colonel's mouth to the congregation; her voice much bigger than her body. I tried to write everything the Colonel was saying. I wasn't sure it was because I was afraid to look at her boots or that every word she spoke was striking good chords in me. I was really happy. Maybe it was my time and season. I couldn't say exactly how. It was simply a maybe.

"When you get back, pack your things. You're being moved to the Headquarters Command Group. I don't know for how long but your presence is wanted immediately."

The Sergeant spoke rapidly. I couldn't tell if he was excited or I was in trouble. I wasn't ready because I couldn't discern the situation. I panicked and tried not to release my fear over the Internet. I was about to respond to the email but decided against it.

The commander was breathing rapidly. It must have been a wonderfully long day for him or we were about to encounter upon an exciting "vacation deal". I hurried to my tent and started to pack. Two senior soldiers came to give their support. I was completely packed and gone within an hour. I stumbled over my prayer and afraid to ask about the situation.

I had helped so many people along the way. Now it was my turn to "go through". I was frightened and couldn't think of any advice for myself that I had given to others. My past thoughts came to present.

I thought about my patience with Private Rudan. I thought about why I was there. I drew a blank. I needed to know how to discern the times. There is indeed a reason, a purpose, and a time for everything. In my thoughts, the ride for Private Rudan pulled into the parking lot.

"Should you be here?" I looked at each of the senior soldiers who came into the tent.

"Yes, we can be here. We're helping you." The senior or them spoke. He strolled confidently about the tent with ease and poise. Although we were in the desert, his unformed was as crisp as a garrison soldier. His tall, lean frame made the tent appear smaller. He snapped out instructions to the other soldiers. Immediately they packed and picked up footlockers and boxes and moved expeditiously out of the tent and quickly returned. I partially packed, partially thought about my career and partially blanked out. I can't remember loading all of my equipment. At that moment it mattered little.

"There's a purpose, a season, a time for everything. God is overseeing the events of our lives."

I listened. I heard. I couldn't fully believe. If God was overseeing the events of my life, why was I going through the pains of disrespect and deceit? I was growing and I dared not ask Him. In my mind, tears rolled down my face. I wanted them to flow freely in reality but decided against it. My time had come I agreed. It just wasn't a good one for me. But I vowed that I would be strong and not pluck at my victory. The scripture had not changed. *All things work together for good.* Today I really believed that. About three years ago I wasn't so sure. I felt great knowing and understanding God has a perfect plan. Though my heart ached, I stayed focused.

"Don't stay focused on the calamities of the world. Don't stay stuck on the "ugly". Remember God is…"

Far away? That day I felt like God was too far away for me to cry out to Him. I didn't realize it was my season and time. I wasn't ready at all. God knew that I wasn't. *Ecclesiastes 3:1-9. To everything there is a season…a time…a purpose… A time to… What do I do? I Chronicles 12:32…the children…had understanding of the times to know what to do.*

I wasn't going to know what to do. I definitely didn't totally understand my time. However, I knew I wasn't ready.

"We're stuck on the "why". We need to remember that God is. Turn to Ecclesiastes 5:15 Redeeming the times for days are evil… Be careful and make the most of every opportunity because the times are evil. If you take time and think about the times you're in, you could actually reap benefits in the most uncomfortable situations."

That was a lot said in one breath. I watched the Colonel come from behind the pulpit. I quickly shut my eyes. I still hadn't looked at her boots. I was still afraid. The sermon was too powerful. I put my attention back on the Colonel. I was sure to look at her upper body only. I cringed and wrote. I wrote verbatim to keep my eyes off of her boots. They're desert tan I reminded myself.

"Be sensitive to the moments and stay on track. Wait for redemption. God will purposely tear us down, get us out of sync and then give us time to orient ourselves. However, He can only give way to redemption if you let go of the way things used to be. Don't resist transition. Don't mess up the flow. Stay focused and connected." The Colonel took two steps back and two deep breaths.

My heart was full and my mind felt heavy. I tried to write all of the critical scriptures and notes. It was more so that I couldn't see her feet and less so I could go back to them. I'd remember so that was not the case. I wanted to revisit the sermon but I already knew when I reached for it, it would be in my head.

Colossians 4:5-6…be wise and make most of every opportunity. Let your words be full of grace.

Luke 19:41-44…had you only known that this day would bring you peace. But you didn't know it was a sign of God coming to you.

Jesus said to us, "It is Me."

I fazed out of my reflective state to hear the Army preacher continue with her sermon. I was so involved in my reflection that I forgot about the golden shoes. There stood the preacher on the floor just below the pulpit. I raised my head to the level of her boots. I am sure I screamed out loud when I saw the golden boots setting at my eye level. I was sure someone heard my scream.

It startled me! I looked to my left and my right. No one appeared alarmed or frazzled. The boots were fiery golden and I was sure I wasn't the only one who saw them. I was not ready to see the symbol. I couldn't figure out its meaning. A floating preacher and a set of golden shoes worn by the divine elite; I was ready for my time.

The sermon!

There's a purpose, a season, a time for everything. The devil wants us to focus on the calamities of the world. Don't let him win your heart and soul. Remember God is overseeing the events of our lives. Stay focused on God's works.

Regardless of the reflection of today's sermon, I still wasn't ready. I understood. I just didn't feel like I was ready.

We arrived at my new place. The same soldiers helped me to unload all of my equipment. I had unconsciously packed a few of my senior soldier's videos. I promised myself to give them back later. I had more gear than I'd originally thought. Nonetheless I sadly unloaded the vehicle and placed it in my new surroundings. I was going to count the number of trips to and from the vehicle. It wasn't helping me to feel better.

I cried inside knowing that it was my time, season and purpose. I choked on my words. I wanted to ask "why?" I told myself that this was a new beginning. I was in the process of taking every opportunity to get closer to God and make every effort to understand the will of my Father, God. And of course, along with His perfect plan.

I walked in the gravel and sand to get another handful of my things. I would organize it later. Some of the stuff I had really didn't get used but I didn't want to get rid of it and need it later. Almost like when people think they don't need God. They ditch Him and then call on Him later. Much of the stuff I needed I didn't have. Again, I don't want to be in a position where I am calling on Jesus but He doesn't answer because I knew I needed Him but fail to believe in His word. My time, season and purpose. I didn't see it coming. I made six more trips to and from the vehicle. The soldiers drove away leaving me to start fresh in the morning greeting a new unit.

"Don't hold on to the way things used to be. Don't resist transition. Stay focused and connected. Stay on track for redemption. Don't hold fast to old stuff."

I found the card with the Colonel's phone number and office number. I was slightly familiar with the lay out of the new installation. I decided to ask directions from the first soldier I passed if I started heading in the wrong direction. I always made plenty of time to get where I needed to go. So, I planned to walk slowly in order to take in my new surroundings.

I stood in the middle of my new residence missing my own camp. I missed the unpredictability of the sand storms and the daily malfunctions of the air conditioners and shower points not having sufficient water. I missed the long chow lines and the crowded gym. Walking through the neighborhood of the new installation made me laugh about the times I would get ready for a shower and there was no water. I'd have to use a few water bottles or wait it out until the afternoon. It was the desert so who cared?

I laughed out loud also when I thought about how everyone came flying out of the tents one afternoon when the air went out. If we needed to call an emergency formation all we had to do was shut off the air conditioner and you'd see hundreds of troops out front. I also ate a lot of sand at my old camp. I couldn't wear my cocoa butter skin cream or chap stick. If I did wear it, sand would get stuck on my lips and face. I just never knew when a storm was coming so I had to carry my scarf and stay ready. Those small things in retrospect were actually pretty funny and all of a sudden, I realized that I liked them. Even trying to predict when to chew gum.

Now, I had to let go of those memories and put some focus on my new job. Morning for me would come quick. I returned to my room and began sorting my things.

Don't hold on to the way things used to be. Move on and accept the transition. My new job; whatever that might be.

"Turn your Bibles please to Matthew 24:36-39." The pause was natural and it gave us time to find the scripture. "These scriptures or verses, if you may, tell you why you shouldn't hold on to old things. The way things used to be. The way you want things to be in *your* mind. Matthew 24:36-39 tells us that no one knows when the time and season is over. Not even the angels in heaven."

That was a bit of a relief. I used to think that God had a plan so perfect and secret and we (the humans) were the only ones who knew nothing about it. I now know that God's *own* angels didn't even know. Sometimes it's just not good for everybody to know everything.

"Do you have a few words to say?" The Commander stood next to me and waited for me to finish my few words.

"I am honored," I begin in my most professional tone, "that the United States Army has found great valor, honor and entrusted me with a higher rank to continue serving my country. To continue to mold soldiers like you into soldiers like myself. The Army has also seen fit to give you a greater challenge to mold me into the best officer the Army has to offer." I smiled and motioned that my speech was done. I didn't have much to say. I was happy about my promotion, just not real wordy about it. Then it was the Commander's turn to speak. He stepped in front of me. I took a few steps back to give him space. He put the unit at ease and began his speech.

"Good morning to all of you. I am indeed honored to award this fine soldier a rank of greater responsibility. She is doing a fine job and we wish her well." He paused and the unit readied to applaud but he wasn't quite finished with his speech. He took a deep breath and continued.

"As you all well know the government is trying to get units home early. We could be out of here well before Christmas." The unit cringed, eyes bulged and hearts raced at the sound of the good news. I made no reaction because I felt that wasn't a good piece of information to give out right then and being a part of the Army for the time I have. Just not a good idea. Everybody just didn't need to know everything right now. I pictured soldiers fighting for telephone space to call home and say, "We're going to be home on December 18. We can go to grandma's for Christmas!" "The Commander just told us that we are leaving because there're too many of us here?" "Honey, go ahead and book that trip to Disney, I'm going to be able to go with you guys".

That's why God's angels didn't know and especially us. How could He ensure that no one would tell? How could we ensure that the true date and time of Christ's return was the right date? Who would pass of the information, the right information?

Like Noah, I needed my new rank to have leverage.
"Noah didn't know when the storm was coming, but he was commanded to be ready. He was instructed to build a boat in the desert for a flood that was on its way. The people didn't believe him. He was told to get rid of the old and prepare for the new. God placed Noah and all the people in position for a transition. Some accepted, others laughed that it could never be true, and even others just failed to listen. The people were placed in their season and time. But they didn't get focused. They didn't prepare. The flood came and took them all away."

I thought about whether or not I had signs shown to me. I couldn't remember. I sifted through my belongings trying to get myself together before morning. I bagged my unneeded items and placed them in the bottom of my footlocker. I hadn't used that stuff in six months. Useless. I tried not to cry again. I had cried a lot before the move just because of what I thought I was going through. I had used a lot of tears in the past and had overcome all that in the few months. I needed to be strong for me. I could do it all again. I had to get ready and position myself for a transition.

Was all that crying over someone else's deeds worth my energy?

It wasn't.

"You may not believe me when I tell you that God has got this. God places you in a better position for your condition. If you don't believe me when I tell you, turn to Corinthians 2:6-16."

The golden shoes had my attention yet I still heard the preacher clearly. My eyes welled with tears. I still couldn't understand the symbolism of the golden shoes, boots in this case. I was open to God to tell me in His own time. I wrote like I knew what the next words were going to be. I knew that I really needed to remember what God had to say to me.

"In I Corinthians the second chapter we are told that God has revealed things to us by His spirit. No eyes have seen. No ears have heard. No mind knows what God has prepared for those who love Him. For those who stay focused on His work. Stay on track and wait for redemption. Let go of the way things used to be. Don't ever grab hold of the things that you think ought to be. God is overseeing the events of our life and He will not fail us."

I allowed my heart to stop crying, I had a job to do. God has placed me in a season of time. I knew I wouldn't see a bright green two-piece dress suit or pants suit this Sunday. It was 1800hours (that would be six o'clock in the evening). I hoped not to see any pairs of golden shoes, slippers, sandals, nothing golden.

The video projector belted out sweet soft words of worship. I'd never heard either of the songs before, but I felt the joy in them just as much. The Colonel walked up to the pulpit. She didn't take a seat. She pressed on the front pockets of her crisp uniform. I guessed she had several of them. The past few Sundays she stood at the left podium but had gradually moved to the middle of the long pulpit.

The pages rustled as they were being turned to II Timothy 2:15. A commitment to ministry. Be encouraged and stay on track waiting for redemption during your transition. Much easier said than done.

Chapter Seven

A Letter of Encouragement

The next morning wasn't as hustling and full of anxiety as the days on the old camp. The cellular phone wasn't ringing at 0800 hours (that is eight o'clock in the morning) asking questions about the day's operations. No one was greeting me for the day and this new camp felt congested because of all the troops present. I was greeted but not by many.

It was a very different atmosphere. I considered it a true transition. I'm usually a happy person but today I needed a word of encouragement. I needed someone, anyone, to tell me it was going to be fine. Today I was in my time and season; unprepared. I didn't like it but I knew I had to face it. A peek at the golden shoes would set my heart at ease I thought. They meant something spectacular. I wanted to know. I had to go through this transition if I was to find the answer. When I did find the answer, what would I do with it? While I am looking for it, what should I be doing? I needed to be encouraged and stay in the fight. I think that's what I was supposed to do in this time and season?

"Remember when you're experiencing trials that God won't send you anything Jesus died to deliver us from. God won't send sickness and tragedy. God won't send destruction and hatred. God won't send you through frustration and confusion. God won't send you through heartache and pains with no end and no reason. God ain't in it if you can't get through it".

That was what I had to go by to encourage me; *"God ain't in it if you can't get through it"*. Now I understand that God won't leave me alone. I walked down the paved street. The soldiers and vehicles shared the road. As I walked, I noticed how the soldiers and vehicles worked together to share the road. They were committed to safety.

I heard the last of the pages. I glanced up to see the Colonel pausing before reading.

"… a workman that needeth not to be ashamed, rightly dividing the word of truth. Do what you can to represent the body of Christ. Tell others of God's good work. Commit yourself to doing what's right. Be disciplined leaders. We tell our soldiers all the time to recite the definition of discipline: doing what's right when no one is watching. We must obey God and stay encouraged."

What does the scripture say about encouragement? Who was speaking in II Timothy the second chapter and whom was he saying it to? How does II Timothy apply to me? I peeked at a few of the verses. I didn't hear the Colonel. I wanted to know how I could be encouraged and stay committed.

Avoid godless chatter because it will only get worse. It will spread like an infection destroying good things along the way. God's foundation stands firm and is not garbled up by the evil words of them. Don't listen, don't speak, and don't participate. I was encouraged in my heart. I just needed to displace it outward. I needed to action my encouragement.

I stayed on my side of the road and continued to watch the soldiers and the traffic. When we're in trials, ask God for wisdom and perspective on the situation. What can I do? I can stay on one side of the road allowing the vehicles room to maneuver around me. We can't always be in control of our situation but we can control our response. A vehicle whipped by me on the left. It startled me. I moved closer to the parked vehicles. I wasn't angry with the driver. I was in control of my responses. I walked the rest of the paved road watching carefully for speeding vehicles as well as vehicles in general. I stayed committed and still in need of encouragement. Perhaps the golden shoes were a symbol of peace. When I saw them, I paid attention immediately blocking out all else around me. I wasn't for sure how. It was a start.

Another car whizzed by. I stepped toward the place that could have been the sidewalk and showed no anger.

"Turn with me to the book of Job. Let's glance at Job. Many of us know the story of Job." I watched the Army preacher gleamed with excitement. She was still serious about her message but I could tell she was excited about the story of Job. Who wouldn't be? I admired Job. He was a man that God found to be upright. Job was like my mom, faithful even in the midst of a calamity. My mom was poor. That meant we were poor too. My mom was a happy poor mother and wife. I'm sure God found favor in her.

I took a peek at the shoes and put my attention on the preacher.

"We know in the midst of Job's trials, he said some things. Job 1:21, Job spoke of his fear. Job 3:25, God will take what He gave me. What I feared is here. What I dreaded has happened. My peace and rest have been taken. Now I must suffer. II Timothy 3:16. No one came to support or defend me. But the Lord came and I was delivered."

Powerful words spilled from the mouth of the powerful Army preacher. Yes, I was familiar, very familiar with the story of Job. The preacher retold the story in a way that had the members on the edge of their seat. Stay encouraged. If Job did it, then I certainly could. I didn't have half to contend with in comparison to what he bore. I wrote in my notebook. I used half a page of notes. Interesting. A letter of encouragement. Job wrote none but his story tells all.

We are in control of our response, feeling and processing of a situation. We control how we think. How can we be encouraged? How can we be of encouragement?

"II Peter 1:20," continued the Colonel, "tells us the prophecy from God is spoken by man through the Holy Spirit. No prophecy of the Bible is left without interpretation."

The chapel grew silent for a few seconds. No praise phrases bounced about the congregation. I held tight my pen and waited for the next stack of information. All I could remember was, "But the Lord came and I was delivered".

I started thinking like Job in some regards. Job wanted to know what he could do to help his situation. Lord, what can I do to help my situation? I began to write my own letter of encouragement. The first sentence would tell me to stay committed to the ministry of saving my soul and the souls of others. The second sentence had not yet surfaced.

I walked into the parking lot of my new building. I couldn't imagine not working in a tent. I stood in the parking lot staring at the building referred to as a hardstand. When you're in a trial for God's sake try to focus on what you can do. Ask for wisdom and perspective.

"Why did Paul say what he did in his second letter to the church? The letter served as an urgent request to the people." The Colonel paused. She looked directly at me. I shivered. She couldn't have known I needed encouragement. We all need to be encouraged. I stared at each crease in her uniform. I was afraid to drop my eyes a little to see if her feet were touching the floor. The eye contact felt like eternity. Her feet were planted firmly on the pulpit floor. I looked down to give a closer attention to her boots. I sort of knew what would happen. I was the only one who could see them or at least I thought I was the only one. I was too afraid to ask anyone else. Clay never believed me so who else would?

Her next sentence should have broken my trance. I wanted to leave today encouraged.

The first day in an office inside a hardstand was weird. I was thirty pounds gearless and nervous about using more technical skills than tactical. I was escorted to the nearly empty office and given a broad operation to decipher and make sense. I had no real idea about how I would pursue this monster. I did know that encouragement, wisdom, and perspective would be my greatest help.

"Major Scottsville." The voice rang through the halls. I wasn't startled. As a matter of fact, it sounded rather non-military. It was pleasant.

I was certain to respond with "Sir". I noticed I was the lowest ranking person in the building.

"Yes, Sir." I hoped my voice wasn't shaky. It was.

"Are you the officer from Camp Newyat?" The rank was big and black. Lieutenant Colonel. I immediately assumed the position of attention. Sweat was rolling down my back.

"Yes, Sir," I repeated. The few officers gathered went about their day. I assumed it was a cue that he wanted privacy time with me. I wasn't sure if I was to leave or stay. I waited to see what he was going to do. I leaned in just slightly to read his nametape, Brouxett. I pronounced it Broc-ket in my mind. I'm sure my lips moved.

The last of the officers dispersed. I remained at attention.

"Sir, Lieutenant Colonel Brew-K (Brouxett). I am to see you when I report, Sir."

Another Lieutenant Colonel named Brochet walked by me. I hoped I wasn't to see this officer but the other one. More sweat came. Encourage my soul I prayed. I waited a few seconds. The Lieutenant Colonel waved his hand where I stood and went on his way. I went on my way as well. No direction, no instruction, no task. I went to my empty office and sat. If I had a letter of encouragement, I would have pulled it out and read it at that moment. Maybe it was a sign for me to start writing one. That would be a great beginning. I still needed to know what to do in my time and season.

A young soldier stopped by my make shift office.

"Hey Ma'am, can you tell me where I can find Lieutenant Colonel Brochet?" He pronounced it Brew-K as well. I felt a bit relieved. He was a tall thin Master Sergeant wearing a crisp uniform. His uniform was donned with Airborne, Air Assault, Drill Sergeant, and Recruiter insignias and badges. I wondered if he needed encouraging. I smiled at him as to show my pleasantness and not my newness to the job.

"To your immediate right, down the hall. It's the first office on the left. Let me know if you need much else Master Sergeant." The Master Sergeant smiled and thanked me. I felt important at that very moment. The second sentence of my letter was beginning to form.

The entire day in the hardstand was long and boring. I wasn't use to not getting called every few hours. I wasn't use to not checking on the camp's security all day. I decided my new position wasn't accidental but prophetic. It was boring yet meaningful. It was less stressful and more spiritually demanding. I pulled out some paper and wrote the first two sentences of my letter of encouragement. My first sentence addressed the need for encouragement. My second sentence explained that it was my season, time, and purpose. I needed to be encouraged committed and prepared to take on the task. I was indeed the new officer in town. The next challenge would be my third sentence. What was I to do?

Now, what *was* my purpose? Where *am* I in the mix? I looked about and started to write. I wrote in an attempt to encourage myself…

For reasons unknown I didn't realize until the following Sunday what I was to put as my third sentence. I was happy to know that not only was there a way to survive a satanic attack but also a way to encourage myself in any situation. This was indeed a powerful Sunday.

I watched her once again walk across the pulpit. The blaze from her golden boots spread from the front of the chapel to the seventh pew: my row. I opened my mind to accept the Word of God this evening. I readied my materials and my spirit. The Colonel took her rightful place in the small pulpit. There was another minister seated and the tall Staff Sergeant stood at the podium giving the initial praises to God. Her voice was soft and sincere and her spirit was wide open for Christ. She hummed and waved her hands as the last words of the worship song touched the congregation.

"Give God some praise," the Staff Sergeant shouted in a soft voice. "Give God some praise tonight. Some members had remained seated. Some stood. I stood as well. I had learned through the years and during my desert experience that God deserved all of my praise. There was a point in my life that I wondered why but tonight I needed that boat. I needed that boat although I was in the desert. I was anxious to find out or hear my reason for building a boat in the desert. I was sure, as long as I opened my heart to Christ so that I'd understand why and be prepared to survive. There was a way and there was a purpose and I was in a season of…

The Colonel approached the pulpit. I discovered I'd already missed something. "Stay ready Coriander. You just never know when so stay ready." I looked into the Colonel's heart. What would she tell me today to help me continue to add on to my boat. Her mouth opened.

"Saints, saints, saints," she looked into the congregation. I looked at her and then at the cross that was set up in front of the podium. It was crooked. I thought about Christ and how He works so hard to keep us straight. He had to lean in our direction to help us out of all kinds of situations. "Saints," she said once more. "The song we just worshipped to is exactly what we need to do. Trust His heart when we can't touch His hand. Did you realize that *nothing* takes God by surprise? We think that just because we're going through, God takes a break. God works just like Satan. He doesn't take breaks. How can He when the devil never takes one? But we don't realize that now do we? Turn with me if you will to I Thessalonians 5:18-23. I think I need to tell you what you need to do when you're going through your season, your time, standing on top of your purpose. I feel like the Spirit is telling me to tell you how to be on your A game. So go with me to I Thessalonians 5:18-23. I Thessalonians 5:18-23." She repeated three times. I had time to write it down and turn to it. I stood again as the Colonel read the words from the Bible. "In everything…

I watched her. I thought I saw her in a black robe floating across the pulpit. The cross was still crooked. I went south on the sermon. Now where was I on my construction? Where did I stand in Christ and still what could I do when I got in a situation? Where was I in Christ?

Yet another question was keeping me from working my way out of a situation. My letter of encouragement…

Chapter Eight

WHERE ARE YOU IN CHRIST?

"Today's meeting is to scrub the contact list. Just in case we have an event, incident, or what have you, you or at least the duty officer will know who to contact."

"Is this the same as the one we use at Group? If so then we should all be in order."

The uncertainty in the sergeant's voice led me to believe that all wasn't so in order. I fished about the office to get a contact roster. I located one and began to go through the names on the list with the unit points of contact (POC), then by single movers then by the staff members present. There were about three names not listed and I didn't recall seeing the 8158th Transportation Company. I wanted to say something but I didn't feel like I was in the right position to make the corrections. I had only been on the job five days. I sat staring at the roster. Here I was in a unit and didn't know where I stood.

I was banned from my home unit for reasons unknown to me. Yes, I was told my presence was requested and I accepted that because it sounded better. I knew that wasn't the case. I was doing a great job where I was. Why would I be requested to move? I concluded that it was my time. I missed going to choir rehearsal and learning new songs.

Tears rolled down my heart.

I took two deep breaths and reminded myself to be encouraged. I was on a mission to find myself in Christ.

This particular Sunday the high ranked chaplain stepped into the pulpit dressed in a two-piece pants suit. The dark purple did well for her hairstyle, skin complexion, and overall spirit. I smiled to see such a woman after God's own heart. I smiled as I scanned the congregation. Four seats up from where I sat was a lady with a real church hat. I felt like I was at home. The black hat was decorated with a wide white band across it. It seemed very big inside the church surrounded by soldiers. I even took a few seconds to check the shoes and boots of some of the church members. No one had on golden shoes or boots.

The very presence of the hat took away the thoughts of the war. I took more time to look around. It was indeed an "at home" kind of atmosphere, but without my family. I remembered how when we were children, Ellery used to talk about the ladies' hats. I would laugh so hard we'd get in trouble by my mom.

Now my own children did the same thing when we went to church.

"Mom, are we going to church tomorrow? Today is Saturday. Tomorrow is Sunday. Are we going to church?" The pant legs covered my son's shoes. His shirt was huge. I wondered if his pants were pulled up all the way. He pranced about the television room and turned a few flips. His happiness made me feel like I was a part of something wonderful. I knew my specific place as a mother. I just needed to work a little more on my place in Christ. That was my plan.

"Yes, sweetie. We go to church tomorrow. Are you going with me?" I looked over my shoulder in time enough to catch my son taking a nosedive on the staircase. He began to cry. I moved quickly and picked him up. His loud cry hurt my heart more so than the possible bruise he sustained. I rubbed his hands and face. At age seven, he was still my baby.

"You need to be careful Elmon. This isn't the park. We're in the house." I wiped his tears and rubbed his hands a bit.

"Yes, I'm going with you tomorrow," he told me between tears.

I smiled. I looked around the house. This is where I belonged. I belonged here taking care of my husband and my children. I smiled again and Elmon stood up and went about his way. I knew he'd return later and try to jump the staircase.

I rose to return to whatever it was I was doing. Perhaps preparing dinner.

Another voice rang through my home.

"Mom, mommy!" The high pitch sound of desperation was Davel, another one of our children needing me. I dashed from the kitchen and went to find the voice.

Where are you in Christ? The question floated from the pulpit into the congregation and perhaps out of the church doors into the streets. Where are you in Christ?

"Turn with me to Proverbs 11:24-25 ... scattereth ... and yet increaseth ... withholding more than is meat. The liberal soul shall be made fat ... your position in Christ will increase as you put more into it. You can learn and grow where you are and where you're going in Christ. If you don't know God, we'll show you."

The soldiers paused and slowly walked across the chapel pulpit. I watched straining to take in her every word. I didn't anticipate her boots. I could already feel the golden color screaming at me. I wrote, prayed, and listened.

"Christ guards your heart. He does so to give you strength to know your place, get in your place and work your position." I recognized that advice from Pastor Leonard. Know your place. Get in your place and stay in your place.

The chaplain took another pause and walked a little more across the pulpit. I didn't need to write what was said. I was familiar with trying to find my place in life. The road to that place was…

"Yes, sweetie." My oldest son's face was draped with frustration and grief. I watched the rapid rise and fall of his chest. Something was exciting him but it wasn't a good kind of excitement. I looked about his half tidy bedroom. I saw his math book opened on the floor. Math wasn't his favorite subject. Neither was it mine, so I was able to relate.

"I have to get my homework done and I need help." He struggled to hold back his tears.

It was my place to keep everything in perspective. I walked toward his sprawled school materials.

"Come sweetie. Let's get your work done. I'd like to relax. Deal?"

Davel organized his books as they lay on the floor. I watched him as he flipped a few pages. He wore his favorite jeans and T-shirt. I wanted him to wear his other clothes but we didn't discuss it because he was doing well in school. We agreed that so long as his grades were decent and he took responsibility of getting ready for school each day then he could wear what he liked. He did just that. He kept decent grades and he wore his favorite clothes.

I read the directions aloud, slowly. I read them once more. I did one of the problems, explaining as I calculated. We did the next one together. I still explained step by step. I had my son do a problem independently and then had him explain it to me. He smiled because he could do the problem.

"Here's how you check your answer." I wrote one of the problems, solved it and checked it. Davel smiled signaling that he was able to go it alone. I had done my part and he was ready to step in his place and complete his assignment. I rose from his books and headed back to the kitchen.

I didn't always know where I stood. I didn't always know what my family needed. They showed me what they needed.

"If you don't know, God will show you."

"I Timothy 5:17 assures us that a way has been provided for us. There is a way by which we will know our place in Christ. The elders give the method to us. The elders are responsible for preaching and teaching. The preacher paused and look quickly about the congregation. He wanted to say more. I held my breath and waited for it. "Saints, as a parent, you are responsible for preaching and teaching your children. You are responsible for the direction and guidance you give them." He continued and I thought about my own girls and how it was so very important to me that they were well taught and giving reliable guidance. Mylene, a beautiful young lady preparing for an ugly adulthood, needed me. I had to be there for her. She'd need me for a long leg of her journey. I was sure of it. I returned my attention to the preacher. I was just in time to hear him tell the church.

"God will show you where you need to be. You will make sure you stay there in good operation."

I blinked and wrote the sentences in my notebook. We're all equally important in some fashion. We have a place in Christ as we do in our homes and on our jobs. We are taught everything we need to know about our new position. After a while it is our responsibility to maintain the skills and progress. In our family we are told or showed family expectations. It is up to us to keep the love in the house.

Where am I in Christ? How can I get there and how can I stay there? My power was running low. Like one of my troops would say "my oil light came on". My oil light was blinking furiously and I wanted to make sure I was ready for the storm. Noah was told to build an ark so that when the flood struck the earth, he would be ready. Noah took to God's instructions. He had what we work to keep daily: faith. Noah had faith in God and what God could do. God showed no evidence as to His plan. Noah trusted God and kept the faith. In the terrible situation God place Noah and Job, they both did something to make it through. I know that they had faith but they also were encouraged.

I wanted what Noah and Job had. I wanted to able to use the evidence of faith to be thankful and stay plugged into the power source of God. But first I had to hold on to the understanding of my place in Christ. Keeping the faith.

Chapter Nine

EVIDENCE OF FAITH

How can I stay where Christ puts me? I work hard keeping my family together.

My girls decided to come by for a visit. The same day, a Saturday, my sisters and brother, came too. The atmosphere was as usual; loud and cheerful and crowded. I smiled to myself knowing that I had a lot of work to do.

"Coriander, bring me a pop!" My sister yelled from the family room out in the garage.

"She can get that herself."

"Don't worry about it." The Motivator kissed my forehead and went outside. "Just let it work. It'll work itself out."

"What's that supposed to mean?" I followed the Motivator.

"Coriander, where's my pop?" asked my third sister.

"Bring me one too," said my baby sister.

I smiled on my way to the refrigerator in the garage. I picked out a really cold grape and orange pop.

I laughed out loud, "Coming". I quickly took up all the stairs and leaped into the family room. I almost knocked down my youngest daughter on the way.

"Hi, sweetie." Javon stood over the last steps. She wore a set of jeans and a fancy blouse. Her hair was braided in about one hundred braids. Her face was smooth but bore no make-up. She was still as pretty as she was when she was a baby. I was happy to see her because since she'd been an adult, we didn't see her much. She'd stop by periodically for a few minutes and then head out. Her trips to the house basically consisted of coming to see her brothers and nephews and nieces. I was sure she was on her way somewhere when we bumped into each other on the staircase.

"Hi," she laughed. "Your sisters are calling you. You better get in there." She laughed some more.

"That's not funny. Where are you headed?"

"Down the street, but I'm coming back to eat. You cooked right?" She headed out the door. She didn't wait for my response. She already knew. Just let it work. I smiled and hurried inside before my name was called again.

"Here you go. Please remember to throw the can away. Thanks."

I knew while I was making the request that the can would remain out of the trash until I policed it up.

"We got this. We know what to do. Is the food ready? I hope you fixed more than just hotdogs. We're at your house." Roesander fixed her cream-colored sleeveless blouse while she spoke. She pulled on her Tommy jeans. "I'm hungry. You 'bout done?" She waltzed up the stairs into the kitchen.

"Give me a few minutes. Are the kids going to eat first?"

"Yeah, I'll help get the plates fixed".

I watched Ellery slowly move about the kitchen. The doorbell rang. I thought about the times when we were much younger. I laughed to myself to see her in a jogging suit. She was still Ellery. She wore a jogging suit, not a totally marvelous outfit just a simple dark colored suit. Who would've though it? She slowly pulled the paper plates from the counter. I stepped into the kitchen doorframe to watch her. Ellery counted out about twelve plates.

"Coriander!"

I jumped at the sound of my name. It wasn't that it was yelled out but rather the fact that I went about the house like a hostess. On my way back downstairs, I met Mylene midway. She smiled and waved for me to handle the business at hand. She'd get to talk with me later. She understood and I was glad to see her. I stepped into the kitchen.

"Yeah, Ellery, what you need?" I was so happy. I looked about my kitchen. This was my favorite time. Though it's always a constant rush, I enjoyed it. I was where I was supposed to be. I just let it all work for me. I was on my way to allowing the Word of God to do just the same. It was time to eat.

"Hey guys, come on. It's time to eat," I yelled up and down stairs. Before I could say it again, my other sisters came into the kitchen. Roesander, Rafia, and Gramesheas rolled into the kitchen atop each other. They were screaming and clawing at each other. I had to laugh when Ellery slapped them with her stack of paper plates. The Diva team quickly piled their plates and headed back to the television room. I waited for the next command.

"Coriander, can we get a pop?" It was Roesander's voice. "Didn't I see Mylene somewhere around here?" she added. Rafia and Gramesheas' voice echoed the command. I went to the garage. I picked up the children along the way and escorted them to the table on the way back. Ellery was passing out plates of food. She shuffled from the table to the stove. I made Kool-Aid and mixed it with some ginger ale. Minutes later the house was quiet and everyone was eating. I was thinking. This was my place. I was very sure of it. I rested and took in my surroundings. I only had mere minutes before the chaos would begin again. I smiled and thanked God for this "plan". Take the time to…

"Turn with me to Proverbs 4. Meet me at the twenty-third verse." The preacher paused while the pages turned. I grew into loving to hear the pages of the precious Word turn in unison or staggered. It set the tone for the Word. I pulled out my notebook and a good writing pen. I kept my head down in anticipation of a prayer before getting deep into the sermon.

"If you take time to think about it, God has your best interest at heart. He gives you the strength to supervise what goes in and what comes out of your heart. He gives you the wisdom to shield yourself from danger. He helps you guide your heart." The preacher swayed back and forth. He looked as though he was coming to a conclusion. I paused to be attentive for the title of his sermon.

"Today I'm taking my text from Proverbs along with a few other scriptures to tell you to "Let the Word of God Work for You"."

Another thing I noticed and learned. He was taking his text from several scriptures. He had a main focus scripture and then reference or substantiating text to provide greater meaning and understanding. I was growing. I was learning my position in Christ. Now I would learn to be encouraged and let the Word of God work for me. I took my attention back to the preacher when I thought I heard his voice.

This Army chaplain was not at all like Colonel Groct. He was tall and thick. His bronze skin was shining under the light in the elongated pulpit. His soft voice reminded me of a familiar voice back home. He sounded like an angel. When I heard his voice, I snapped up from my notebook. There was a short silence. I stared at him briefly and returned to my writing when he spoke again.

"Saints, soldier, and friends, Proverbs 4:23-27 tells us to put away corrupt talk from our mouth and lips. Look ahead straightway. Stand on firm ground and stand firm. Don't sway left or right. Find your place and grow."

He was indeed an angel. I was frightened that maybe Pastor Leonard followed me to the desert to keep my mind in motion for Christ. This preacher sounded so much like him. I wanted to know the preacher's name. I couldn't see his nametape from where I sat on the seventh pew. After transferring from Camp Newyat, I still sat in the back of the church. I was able to hear the Word of God. The further back I'd sit the more attention I placed on the preacher to ensure I heard what the Lord had to say to me.

Familiar text. Today I'd learn to do something with what the Word told me.

"Look ahead straightway. Stand on firm ground and stand firm. Don't sway left or right. Find your place and grow."

That was a lot said. I slowly digested the words. I watched the chaplain move about the pulpit. This particular Sunday she wore civilian clothes. Maybe it was a way to get our attention. I watched her move in her two-piece mahogany pants suit. She was attractive in a spiritual nature with a very business look. She reminded all of us about our place and how to stay on track, standing firm. She added her previous plea to discern the times and only worry about the time that we're in, not the time that someone else is in. Let the Word of God work for you when it is your season and time to go through.

I smiled because she was absolutely right. All too familiar.

The mahogany suit strolled to the left side of the pulpit. I did a mental microphone check. I thought maybe I heard her speak. She had said no words. I was thinking of something else. The new chaplain's angelic voice faded.

"Are we going to the park or to the movies?" I wasn't sure if I wanted to do either. I'd be left with the children and my sisters would stay and watch television. I picked up the plates and scraps from the table. I went downstairs to pick up the plates and scraps left by my sisters, brother, and a few of the children. I wanted to pout but decided against it.

"Hey guys, you all want to go to the park?" The happy screams made me smile. I cleared the table. Mylene walked into the kitchen to help. I wanted to see if she'd strike up a conversation. I wanted her to tell me one of those fancy companies called and offered her a job. She was such a wonderful prospect. I almost asked God what was taking so long. I didn't say it and then decided not to speak of it unless Mylene mentioned something first. God was good to all of us. I needed to be patient. I watched from the corner of my eye. Mylene carefully picked up the paper plates from the table and wiped the table and floor. I assisted silently. To break the dark silence, I yelled through the house. "You all get dressed while I clean up. I'll meet you in the garage."

I walked into the garage to get knocked down by the first question.

"Can we ride our bikes?" Elmon stood on the bench looking into my eyes. "Please." I couldn't say yes because everyone didn't have a bike.

"Maybe next time." I gave him a hug and he went on his way.

I replied maybe next time. Elmon took me at my word and moved out. Let the word work for you. It's as simple as an honest response from a child.

"We're ready Tee-Tee."

We all left for the park, all thirteen of us. We knew our place and we let it work for us. I made a habit of having my nieces and nephews along with my other children pair up or get in a line from youngest to oldest. This day I had them in a straight line, "Corn" led the pack and Danielle pulled up the trail. Although Gable was taller, he wasn't older so he still had to walk behind Kazia and Velencia.

Everyone was in his or her place and it all worked.

Mylene blew her car horn as she passed us. She wore an elegant smile. I just hoped her heart wore one in equal size.

The walk to the park was refreshing. I walked behind the line for a bit then on the side. I smiled and though about the Word of God and the sermon I was missing!

The new preacher touched on a few more points then introduced to us Colonel Groct. He had news but he would have an opportunity later to share it with us. This was the second time the chaplain wasn't in her uniform on Sunday. Instead, she wore a black robe with satin red trimming on the sleeves and across the chest. Her feet were covered. The Sunday after this one would be her last Sunday to be in the country. I watched her move about slightly. The red trimming flickered in the dim chapel light. I watched more carefully. I was sure there was a special word from God today. I was sure she was an angelic woman of God. I wasn't so sure I was. I placed all of my attention on her and hoped to not scream if her boots were still golden. I was sure to make preparations to be therefore her farewell Sunday. I wondered instantly if the golden boots would be desert brown by then. She was asked to give parting words.

Her mouth opened. I knew it would be an abbreviated sermon.

"Let the Word work for you." There was a short pause. I took that opportunity to make ready my notebook and good writing pen. She moved from behind the pulpit. I still had my head lifted so I leaned to see her boots.

I can't remember if I screamed or gasped. Her boots were indeed a fiery gold. Her feet were planted firmly but her boots blazed in the dim lit chapel. I looked at the soldier to my right. I wanted badly to ask her did she see the boots.

"Go through when it is your time and season. Discern the times. Don't go through if it ain't for you."

It was my time and season for golden shoes and boots. I must have missed some of what the chaplain was telling us.

"Why is it that we need guidance before we can exercise our trust and faith? We are given a victory and then we pluck it up and ruin that victorious blessing. Then we sit back wondering why we haven't had our prayers answered."

I was guilty of that. In my notebook, I scribbled the sentence about plucking up our victory. It was comical in a way and serious in a lot of ways. I recalled several prayers ago when God took my prayer and was about to dispatch a blessing, but what did I do? I went back to that problem and tried to work on it myself.

I had to get back to the abbreviated sermon.

"Turn with me please," the chaplain stated. The cliché phrase: turn with me please or please stand for the word.

"Turn with me please to Hebrews 4:2. Hebrews 4:2," she paused and walked about the pulpit waiting as the pages were licked and turned. "Hebrews 4:12," she repeated once more. I liked that she repeated the scripture. It gave me time to write it down and look it up.

I did a lot of repeating when I gave out instructions during my teaching career. I wanted to make sure that there were very few questions of the students once they were let out on their own to execute their assigned tasks. The chaplain walked about the pulpit waiting for the last of the pages to turn. I peeked at her golden boots, smiled and went to my own Bible. Parting words.

The Sunday was a joyous one. I walked into the chapel wanting a blessing from the Lord. The members were talking quietly among themselves since there were a few minutes before the service began. I found a good seat in the back and got comfortable. Minutes later the service began. The power projector belted out a praise song. The video showed two small children trying to find their way. I clapped and sang the words I could see on the screen. After all of the singing and greeting we took our seats to prepare to hear a word from the Lord.

Four seats up from where I sat was a lady with a church hat on. It was black with a black and white band across it. The very presence of the hat made me feel at home. I took a moment to look around. It was indeed an "at home" atmosphere. By this time, I had been moved from up north to the south. In the northern camps, very few civilians were employed by the government and lived on the camps with the troops.

At the chapel in the north many of the members wore physical fitness uniforms, battle uniforms, or civilian jogging suits. Several of the soldiers came to the service armed with a weapon and bearing full gear. I did too for the most part. I just wanted to feel safe all the time.

The hat moved which meant I'd missed something. I smiled because I felt at home without my family. I knew God was taking good care of them. I had to because He was doing just that. The sermon just a few Sundays past told me…

"The collecting up of offering will end in two weeks. We were told by the powers that be that we could no longer accept money. So, give today as your heart desires and wait for a blessing."

Offering I thought. I felt more like I was at home. I guess I was going to have to wait until after offering to hear the word. I checked my pockets.

I never thought offering would be collected in a chapel. The fancy trays were passed through the rows. I didn't have any money. The music faded. The Word was about to be rightly divided.

"We have the gospel as did those in the biblical days. The gospel is of no value to us because we have not combined it with faith. God's work is still going on but we claim we need evidence before we can believe or trust God's word. We must have faith and God should be our evidence. Now some of us had the gospel preached and we didn't act on it. I wonder what's that called today."

I was listening attentively. I tried hard to ignore the background noises. I could hear praise phrases, side bar conversations, humming, but no babies crying and no note passing. I was where I was supposed to be and I was gradually learning where I was with Christ. Today I'd add the concept of letting the word work for me. I shook myself to blank out everything except the Word of God. My attention returned to the chaplain.

"It's called disobedience. We are disobedient when we hear the gospel and ignore it. And it tells us... Therefore, God has set aside a certain day, today. Today if you hear, let your hearts be open to receive. The evidence is faith, faith is knowing the gospel."

The chaplain's voice elevated slightly. "By faith we understand. If you're doubtful be patient. Give God time to work." Her parting words.

The praise phrases consumed the congregation. Evidently somebody got the gospel. Somebody was in agreement.

"Speak it."

"Make it plain, make it plain."

"Right, right."

I enjoyed the different styles of praise phrases. They were cute and original. I blurted out one too; tell it all tonight. I wasn't sure if it fit into the scene.

"Give God time and let the Word of Him work for you. I don't think you all are with me. Are you with me? Are we touching and agreeing?"

More praise phrases rang throughout the chapel. I wrote and wrote because this was a sermon worth saving. I even had time to let out my own praise phrase before she began her next sentence.

"Turn to Hebrews 11:3." The chaplain paused and walked about the pulpit to give us time to find the scripture. "Hebrews the eleventh chapter and we'll start at the third verse. Say amen when you have it. Hebrews 11:3. I came to Hebrews eleven. I read verses one and two quickly and slowed down when I came to verse three.

By faith we understand... what is seen was not made out of what was visible. By faith one can please God and without faith one cannot please God. I read more and thought about my own spiritual faith. Did I really trust God to let Him work for me? Was I seeking evidence? I probably was. I would work on my faith. I would work on trusting in God especially in my time and season. I would stay encouraged and see the spiritual evidence of Christ overseeing the events of my life.

My life was good and I guess it always has been. Having faith in God. Now that I knew I just couldn't confirm the calling just yet.

It was a very long time ago.

We sat in the second row trying not to giggle. I looked at Ellery and Roesander. As usual Ellery was dressed for fashion. I smiled at the thought of being in the presence of great company. My family.

The old preacher approached the pulpit. Bishop Peters was his name. I looked up to see Bishop Peters in a tan three-piece suit. Yes, it had been a long time ago. His metallic grey hair lay pressed against his scalp. His dark face shone like a polished copper coin. Bishop Peters didn't sing well so he requested the choir to render an opening selection; Jesus can Work it Out. I loved that song. While the choir sang, I stood up clapping and singing along.

"Jesus can work it out, if you let Him."

"That problem that I had. I just couldn't seem to solve. I prayed and I prayed. Lord let it be resolved. I gave it over to Jesus. I stopped worrying about it. I gave it over to the Lord and He worked it out."

"Oh yes!"

I clapped and sang about how Jesus could work things out. I didn't even know if He could. I wasn't worried about it at the time. I didn't need to I guessed. I continued to clap and sing. Roesander tugged at my dress. When I faced her, she snorted.

"Will you sit down? You're not in the choir. You can't even sing." I would have explained exactly to her why I was singing. I took in her words and her facial expression. I turned my head to ignore her next statement and sang louder.

"Work it out. Work it out!"

"A waste of time," Ellery whispered to Roesander. "That song is old anyway."

It didn't matter to me. It was fitting. I waved at my brother who played the base guitar. He was showing much improvement. I wished for the moment that he could beat up those boys like he played the bass guitar. I was asking in my heart for God to work it out for us. Especially for my brother.

"Didn't He, didn't He work it out? Didn't He didn't He work it out?" I sang it but I couldn't answer the question. I continued to clap and sing. Gramesheas came in during the middle part of the song. We made room for her across the pew and I continued singing.

"Coriander at it again?" I heard Gramesheas ask Ellery and Roesander. She knew something was out of place by the look on their faces. "I hope you didn't ask her to sit down."

"Roesander did," replied Ellery immediately.

"You agreed?" Gramesheas asked Ellery.

"Yep."

"Well, that's why she's singing so loud and off key," Gramesheas laughed. She pressed the back of her skirt and made herself more comfortable. She was almost identical to Ellery in her fashion. She wore a French cut blouse with many of the top buttons unbuttoned. Ellery wore a Tommy blouse with a gold necklace draping on her neck. Gramesheas wore a long satin skirt with high splits on both sides. Ellery wore a rayon skirt with one split on the left side. I could see her three ankle bracelets hanging perfectly on her thin ankle. The divas were just a few years older and still beautiful. They were my sisters and they were beautiful. I smiled and sang along with the choir. I thought about Rafia. She'd be here soon dressed just like my other sisters. I checked the pew to be sure there would be enough room for her.

The choir ended the song and I sat down.

"Thank God," I heard Roesander whisper to Ellery.

"I hope they're not asked to *render* another selection." Ellery had that funny look on her face. I almost laughed out loud.

Shortly before the scripture reading Rafia walked in. She was sharp. Wasn't even embarrassed. I smiled at my baby sister and turned my attention to Bishop Peters.

"Praise the Lord saints," he began. It is indeed a pleasure to stand before you this evening. I am grateful to God for all He has done for me. And thank you choir for that lovely selection for indeed Jesus can work it out for you."

"He needs to work out something on Coriander," Roesander whispered to my sisters.

"Jesus can work it out and you have to have faith and let the Lord work for you." Bishop Peters spoke slowly. He didn't move from behind the pulpit.

Faith.

I just didn't feel like faith was helping us when we started our journey home from school. I didn't need faith, I thought. My brother needed muscles. I hoped for the muscles too. We needed to beat up the children who chased my brother every day after school.

Faith is a big word. Faith allows us to let the word work for us.

Evidence. I came back to the sermon. The days I waited for my brother or ran with him, we needed evidence that God was overseeing the events of our lives. It had been a short long time ago. I tried to fight back the tears of anger.

"Saints, we have to be able to trust God's heart when we can't feel his hands. Nothing that we do takes God by surprise. We complain about things we do, have and don't have. We don't take the time to wait for God's miracle. We want physical evidence before we accept God's power. We want God to show us before we believe. We want to let the word work for us but only in our time. God is overseeing the events of our lives. He will not let us go through what we can't bear. Our tribulations are small in comparison to what God does for us every day."

Praise phrases filled the air. I sat taking it all in. If my sisters were ragging on me, I didn't hear them. Evidence. What is our evidence?

Muscles. I was more concerned about my brother's muscles more so than faith. After hearing Bishop Peters, I felt selfish.

I looked at Roesander, Ellery, and Gramesheas. They had no idea what I was thinking. I was thinking about how much I loved them and where was the Coordinator, Bunny? Bishop Peters continued.

"Let's go to Habakkuk the first chapter and we'll begin at the fifth verse. Please stand for the Word of God." Before everyone stood, Bishop Peters' old voice choked out the scripture.

"...for I will work a work in your days which ye believe not though I have told you." Bishop Peter's voice was old and ragged. He didn't repeat the verse, he didn't wait for everyone to stand and he started reading before everyone got to the verse. The bible pages were still turning in disgust. I heard a few people fussing. I was already at the scripture. I'm sure my mom had already read hers. I looked around to see very few faces in their Bibles.

"Though I told you, you believe me not," he repeated.

I watched Bishop Peters inhale and exhale. He was old. I was hoping he didn't die while rightly dividing the word of truth. I watched his chest rise and fall. He appeared skinny in his three-piece tan suit. His grey hair was laid slick on his head. I took in a few quick breaths myself and stared. He seemed to still in the pulpit. I leaned forward on the pew to see if I could see his chest rising and falling. I didn't want Roesander to get started on me so I didn't keep the lean too much longer. I thought I saw a light coming from the floor of the pulpit so I leaned forward again. I'm sure I had a crazy look on my face. Ellery was already eyeing me and Gramesheas and Rafia were ready to chime in at any moment. I saw a light coming from…

I saw mom looking right in our mouths. I put my attention on the sermon.

"Even if God tells us, we don't believe Him yet we want evidence. We want evidence for everything." I assured myself that there was no light and that Bishop Petters was still breathing. I exhaled pretty loud.

Bunny came in and I was happy to see her. She hustled to the front where mom sat. She settled in and turned to wave at us. I returned a happy wave. My sisters sat like logs. I was just really happy to see her.

"You aren't *that* happy Coriander," snapped Ellery.

"Fake," added Roesander.

I looked at Rafia and Gramesheas to see if they had more to add. I was laughing which I knew would make the situation more irritating.

"I agree with them," Rafia chimed.

"You know what they say," added Gramesheas with a smart tone in her voice.

I laughed. I hoped mom couldn't see or hear me. She'd be furious. I tried to block out the comments in order to hear the word although I still wanted to hear Ellery fussing, Roesander hating, and Rafia and Gramesheas agreeing. It was a beautiful evening.

"Saints, we get upset with God when we have a little faith and no information concerning our prayer requests. What we don't realize is that when we are going through it's only at the blade stage. In other words, we only have a little something working against us."

I watched Bishop Peters' lifeline expand and flow. He spoke quicker and the ragged sound in his voice seemed to have disappeared. I listened closely. A blade size situation. I need to know more about that.

"When you are in your situation, instead of complaining and griping about your little problem you should be thankful." The lifeline expanded more and Bishop Peters leaped with joy. My heart was happy. Yes, my brother had to run every day after school but he always out ran those bullies. He was never harmed and we were always healthy. I smiled and waved at my brother as he played for the preacher.

"Thank you Lord for giving my brother muscles enough to out run the enemy."

I looked at my sisters. They were indeed beautiful ladies. I smiled at them and placed my attention back on the powerful sermon. I know they didn't understand my sudden burst of joy. I smiled at them once more.

"They say she's not wrapped tight," said Gramesheas. I laughed and said thank you. I'll just thank my way out of my blade size troubles.

"Saints we need to thank our way out of our terrible situations. If you thank your way out, you'll realize that the situation was never really all that horrible."

Bishop Peters sounded like a new man. His voice was clear and his words were spoken with much more precision. I hoped he would walk in front of the podium so that I could see his feet. I wanted to determine which time I was in, floating preachers something else. Either way I thought I was ready for it.

He stepped away from the pulpit and I quickly shut my eyes.

Evidently one of my sisters saw me.

"I knew something was wrong with Coriander."

"Maybe she thinks she's an angel or something."

They saw she just plain crazy." I knew for certain that was Gramesheas' comment. I wanted to laugh. I peeked to see where Bishop Peters stood. He had returned to the pulpit. I looked at my sisters who were shaking their head at me.

"Saints, if you turn to Hebrews 6:10 you'll see what the Lord has to tell you." His voice was on a steady rise. The congregation seemed to transition from dull to excitement. I turned quickly to the said scripture and read the verse ahead of the preacher.

God is not so unrighteous to forget your work and labor of love.

I read verses eleven through thirteen to get a better understanding. God was watching over those who worked in faith for His name's sake. Be thankful in the midst of your trials because God was going to reward you openly for your work of love. It was so simple. I smiled openly and readied myself for the diva slashes from my sisters. I could hear them say again, "That child needs some help like now." At that moment, Bishop Peters came from behind the podium. Unprepared. I saw that he was wearing golden shoes!

I was settling in my new position. The supervisor briefly escorted me about the building. I smiled, shook hands and mentally took in names and faces. I wondered who knew me and who didn't. I also wondered if they knew why I'd been transferred. Let the word work for you.

After greeting and shaking the last hand, I was taken back to my office. My supervisor stood in the doorway of the new office.

"Well, that's about enough for the day. Do you have a first name?" The major stood about 6 feet one inch tall. He wore an infantry insignia and he looked the part of a typical infantry soldier. I guessed, from his heavy accent, he was probably from New York or Massachusetts. His voice projection didn't match his size of perhaps 225 pounds or so. I looked up into his ocean green eyes. His extra-long extra thick eyelashes covered his ocean green eyes every few seconds. It was like watching a tide come and go. I didn't know what to say to the massive major.

"Yes sir. That's fine sir."

"Take the rest of the day for in processing. As we discussed you'll work with the engineer detachment. Get with Captain Banks in the morning. He'll instruct you on what needs to be done and what portion he'll want you to do."

"Yes sir." I realized I hadn't answered the question the about my first name. To me, it was a rather ridiculous question anyway. Everybody has a first name so why the question? I think... Just as the major turned to walk away, he asked again, "What was your first name?"

I've always used my last name while in uniform. I hoped I wasn't being a smarty when I replied.

"Scottsville, sir."

"That's your last name," he stated with a strange expression. I couldn't tell if it was a statement or a question.

"Yes sir," I replied immediately.

"You have no first name?"

"Yes sir, I do. I just rather not have it used in this setting. I try to stay professional." I felt sweaty and sounded like I was stuttering. The massive major left my new office. I started to make my office look more welcoming.

Be thankful in the midst of your trials. God will reward you for your work of love.

I made it through the rest of the day and was prepared to return to begin my new position and be thankful about it all.

It had been two weeks since I ran. I felt like I was losing ground on staying in shape. My knees were giving me problems and I wanted to preserve them for at least another six years. I walked around the compound dressed in full armor. I figured I could still stay in shape and preserve my knees too if I walked instead. I stopped after thirty minutes. I was sweating heavily from walking so fast. I might as well have run. I slowed to a stroll to watch the smoke flow from the smoke stacks. I figured I'd return home with something I didn't have before I deployed.

The smoke swirled from the pipes and I pretended to take them in when I inhaled. I watched the smoke circle around the antennas and the few buildings in the area. After a few silent moments, I began the walk back towards my warehouse. I stepped inside the small room. I took inventory of my things. It had been an exciting deployment up to this point. I smiled weakly. I needed to get myself together and move on before I totally lost ground. I put away a few more unnecessary items and decided to call it a night and head to bed.

The day had been a long one and I used most of the day worrying about my reputation. I started thinking about my trial on my job a few years ago. I was so hurt and God seemed so far away at the time. Yet and still, He bought me all the way through. I won that battle but not until I gave it all to Christ and left it there. It was hard for me to do and I didn't want to let it go totally. I kept plucking at it.

God gives us the victory early in our tribulations. We go and pick and pluck at it until it becomes nothing. Nothing but a greater problem.

"I want her gone from this institution. She is not a valuable employee. She should take classes on professionalism and tact."

The words stung my heart. I couldn't believe that someone could say those things about me but they were. The words stung my soul too.

"I'm not sure that you mean all what you say Mrs. Tatred. Mrs. Scottsville is one of our prized employees. You should already know that in all the years you've known her." Great my former supervisor was defending me, my character.

"Well, it is rather sad that I'm the only one who can see through her fakeness and incompetence. It is a sad shame that I have to make these statements openly and you sit there and act as if I'm at fault here. Don't even. She doesn't need to be part of this organization and you well know that. Watch what I tell you!"

I felt myself for blood dripping from my side. Those were hurtful lies and I couldn't believe that one would say such things against me. I wanted to cry right then. I felt like I'd been stabbed. Lord, please help me. Where are You?

In the end the Lord was there all the time. I was rewarded for my work of love. I had actually plucked at my victory that was there in my face, making it into a bigger issue. I had to stop plucking and let God handle it all. When I did, I was victorious. I was growing and I liked where I was heading.

I vowed to stop worrying and just be me and let God work through me. Easier said than done. Let the word work for you I reminded myself. The night was peaceful and full of good rest. I awakened to another blessed day in the desert. I did miss my family and the crazy comments from my sisters. I laughed to think what they'd say about me in my new position. I showered, dressed and headed out to take my ten-minute walk to the hardstand.

I took time to say the Lord's Prayer and thank God for all He does for me. It wasn't all that bad of a situation once I started talking to God. Even in the desert God was there. It was an amazement to know that God could be anywhere in the world. Neat. Devine. Thankful. Blessed.

The day seemed to rush by. I had no time to worry about who knew why I was in a new position and who didn't. They didn't seem to care so I abandoned the thought to concentrate on my new job.

"Okay Scottsville," shouted the massive major. "You should be complete with in processing. Get settled and meet me in my office. I have just the project for you to do." The massive major exited with as much crisp as he had entered. I hurried about the office to make it appear professional. After a half hour, I headed to the major's office.

The office was full of "I love me" artifacts. I took a few seconds to take them all in. I read a few of the certificates that hung on the back of the wall over the desk.

The massive major walked into the office. I was startled.

"Okay young officer here is your first project…"

I was suddenly happy. I allowed my worries to drift out of the major's office into the hallway. Be thankful in the midst I heard the air whisper to my soul.

This was the last Sunday Chaplain Groct preached at the chapel. I was sure to listen to what she had to say. The spirit of the Lord was high and I could feel His presence near me. I refocused. What was the scripture? I looked at my notes I Thessalonians 5:18-23. I read it knowing the Chaplain had read it already. I wasn't supposed to miss this sermon. This was her last Sunday. How could I survive? How could I stay encouraged? I felt the presence of the Lord on my heart. I almost cried when I lifted the words from Thessalonians. There my answer stood in black and white inside my palm sized Bible mom insisted I take and read and use the words to guide me.

In *everything* give thanks. In everything *give* thanks. In everything give *thanks* for this is the will of God concerning you. Hold fast that which is good. I could hear the words echoing. I lifted my head from my Bible. There stood Colonel Groct in her black robe. She was floating back and forth in the pulpit. I could see the blaze of gold from under the robe. She was reading the words from I Thessalonians 5:18-23. I glanced over to see that the cross was straight up, not crooked. I tried to remember if it had been crooked because it wasn't set up right or that… never mind. I placed my full attention on the Army Colonel.

"In everything give thanks for this is the will of God concerning you. Hold fast that which is good. Ignore evil and the very peace of God will sanctify you always. Trust His heart when you can't trace His hand. Nothing I tell you takes God by surprise. God wasn't surprised when the people laughed at Noah. God wasn't surprised when Job's wife wanted him to curse Him and die. Noah and Job were hurt but God wasn't surprised at all. God wasn't surprised when Judeas betrayed His only Son, Jesus. You get the picture. You get into a bind and you have plucked your blessing to ruins and then you say "How am I gonna get out of this mess?" Remember God doesn't make messes. We do. Simple saints. It's so very simple. What does I Thessalonians 5:18-23 tell you to do?" The Colonel walked toward the edge of the pulpit. The praise phrases suffocated the congregation, in a good way. Tears rolled down many faces, hands waved, eyes looked towards heaven, and the presence of the Lord was sucking us in. I tried writing and listening at the same time. I blocked out background noises. My fingers hurt trying to write everything. She spoke fast and truthfully. Here all this time I was trying to find my own way not knowing that had God already made a way. Back to the sermon. The words fell from her lips like butter on a hot roll: steamy and powerful.

"You can experience a break through by saying THANK YOU. If I were to use a text title it would be Thank Your Way Out. Thank your way out of any and every situation. First Thessalonians 5:18-23 tells you to be thankful in everything concerning you for it is the will of God. Now let's go to II Corinthians 4:17." While the pages turned anxiously, the Colonel talked calmly to the congregation. "We are going to see why we just need to thank our way out of a situation. II Corinthians 4:17. Come go with me. II Corinthians 4:17.

Let's see what it tells us." She paused and looked about the congregation. "If you got it say something."

"We're there, preacher."

"Come on ma'am and tell it."

"Praise Him."

"II Corinthians 4:17 tells us that out afflictions are light and only for a moment. God works a work for us far greater than our blade size affliction. Those things we can't see are temporary. Don't waste time worrying about them. Thank God for them and move out. Thank your way out of that situation! Be thankful in all situations for they are small and temporary but God's glory is large and permanent. Are you tracking me? Someone has got to be with me."

"We're there," shouted a member.

"Yes, we are definitely with you ma'am," agreed another.

I agreed as well. I felt like hope came and sat next to me. Be thankful for my situation.

"Okay I Thessalonians 5:18-23 tells us give thanks in everything. II Corinthians 4:17 tells us to be thankful in everything because they're small and temporary. Saints we can't get any better than that. How you gonna get through your situation? Thank your way through. Don't give thanks *for* the situation. Be thankful *in the midst of* the situation. Be thankful *through* the situation. Instead of asking for what you need, thank Him for what you've received and what you already have. I know some of you are probably saying oh preacher that's easy. Thank You, Lord. No. No saints. Want me to add to this thing?"

"Tell it preacher."

"Make it plain, preacher."

"Say it ma'am. Say it."

The black robe moved with the Colonel. It was her last Sunday and she intended to give us some substance we could use for a long time. Why build the boat in the desert? You just never know and you should stay ready. Where are you in Christ? Right here. How can I be encouraged? Be thankful in everything because it's God's will. Be thankful because afflictions are temporary and small. God's glory is great and powerful. Don't let it run out. Can it? I shook at the thought. My problems are as high as the blade under the lawn mower. I have "unkept" weed problems. Can Gd fix those?

"In order to practice and implement your new found information concerning your tribulations you have to have the right attitude. Noah and Job had the right attitude. Albeit afterwards, Judeas got the right attitude. Noah went forward with God's plan regardless of what the people said. Job trusted God. He didn't blame God. He knew God to be a permanent blessing. That he knew. Judeas knew that it was the will of God for him to betray Christ and for that he was remorseful. Nothing can happen to you without God's permission. Believe me Job was not going to suffer long because it wasn't God's doing. God gave the devil permission but it was a temporary affliction mind you." The silence seemed like eternity. I waited. It was so quiet I could hear the people in front of me breathing rapidly. Then the stillness was sliced.

Think for a moment about Abraham. He was going to take his only son and sacrifice him for God. He didn't ask questions and he didn't stall. He just trusted God's plan with all his heart and he obeyed. He thanked God for asking him to sacrifice his son. Amazing. Right saints?"

I wrote as much as I could. It seemed as though the shine from the chaplain's boots grew brighter with each point. I felt like I was squinting but I was still able to see my paper and the pulpit and the preacher making her way back and forth in the pulpit telling me to be thankful regardless.

"Remember that God talks to you always. So, remember what He told you in your darkness when you make it to the light and remember how He protects you in the light when you're in or approaching the dark." She paused for what seemed like several minutes. The piano player eased to the organ. He played a soft song that gradually picked up. I wrote the last sentence and raised my head to the pulpit. Many members were standing to hear the Colonel's last comments on being thankful in everything.

"When you're in the dark you're going to make it to the light. You are afflicted because God's plan is to trip you up to build you up. Cut you back to grow you forward. It's your pruning season. Your situation is working for you not against you. As I come to a close. I want you to close your eyes and stand all over the build." The church stood at her command.

It was quiet though many were praising God. I kept my eyes open looking about the church. I looked at the cross standing straight and strong. Tears began to roll down my face. God had truly been a blessing in my life for thirty-six years. I cried knowing that I stayed in the dark for a short time but most of my entire life has been in the light under the protection of Christ. I begin to understand the boat and the desert and being encouraged and knowing my place in Christ. I saw the evidence of faith in the spiritual and benefited from it in the natural. The tears rolled and I praise and thanked God for my situations. I didn't want to lose the power of God. I wanted so badly to hold on to the faith. I needed more strength. I needed more power. I needed a bigger boat and less desert.

I Thessalonians 5:18-23 and II Corinthians 4:17 would be my temporary power, my starter boat. I felt like there was much more to knowing God than I'd digested tonight. The last Sunday of Colonel Groct guidance left me wondering if…

Chapter Ten

DO YOU REALLY KNOW HIM?

I remember the word "if" from my days of questioning God's plan. I even had a few "what if's" myself. What if God didn't love me? What if I didn't have enough faith? "What if's" could rule my life. I couldn't let them.

I watched the chaplain walk to the pulpit. The preacher in the civilian clothes had introduced him as Minister Reeves. It was Minster Reeves last Sunday in the country. It was my last week in the country. What if I couldn't get my life back together after being away for so long? That was my biggest what if question.

The stage seemed to set farther away this Sunday. I was glad to be able to stay for the entire service. I was working the graveyard shift so my time worked out. I didn't put up a fuss. I let the word work for me and God came through. I quickly thought back on my first Sunday at the new church.

"Are you going to church Scottsville?" The captain smiled and held out his hand for me to shake it. Every time he spoke his first sentence of the day to me, he held out his hand for me to shake it. I took in his small hard hand and smiled.

"I plan to but I'm on the clock right now. I can only stay an hour." I waited for the captain to respond.

Captain Mitlon was a rather older officer. I met him when I was moved into a new position after three months at my previous move. He was about five feet tall. Maybe a few inches but not by much. He had a glowing smile and a very deep southern drawl. He spoke to everyone every morning but I didn't see him shaking any hands. He would go to his desk and then come over to me. After speaking his first sentence, he would stretch out his hand for me to shake it. I like hand shaking so I'd return it with gratitude. He meant well even though he'd ask me several questions a day some of which he'd ask more than once. At first, I was irritated. After a few days I wasn't bothered.

"You're an officer. You can do what you want. Those NCOs will watch the shop." He stepped back to give me space to respond.

"I don't think so. I'd rather just do my hour. I've only been here for a couple days and I'd like to make a good first impression."

"You will. Let's go." Captain Milton reached for my hand and I recoiled.

"Why don't I meet you there."

"You know where it is?"

"No, but I'm sure I can find it." I turned to walk back toward my work area. I hoped the captain wasn't following me. What an irritant I thought with a smile. I watched Captain Milton as he returned to his work area. He looked a bit disappointed.

About a half hour later Captain Milton announced that he was on his way to church. The staff nodded and he left. I waited a few minutes and then announced my departure. The same heads nodded in apparent approval and I left.

The scheduled service was to begin at two fifteen in the afternoon. I walked into the theater. The choir was positioned on the left of the stage. The ministers sat on the right. They were rather far away from the congregation. The theater was packed with soldiers and civilians. I tried to be enthusiastic. I walked quickly to find a pew closer to the back. There were none so I grabbed a chair from the wall and started a new row behind the last row of theater chairs. I probably wasn't supposed to do that but I wanted to be comfortable too. It was fairly warm in the theater. I settled in the chair and watched the events of the service unfold.

The theater was large and filled with lights. I looked about the theater taking in the atmosphere and the congregation. There were a lot of people attending church in the afternoon. I watched as the theater began to fill to near capacity. A few moments later the Captain chaplain approached the podium. His voice echoed across the theater. The chaplain and the ministers and choir still seemed far away, not close like when I come here to watch a movie. Microphones were placed strategically around the choir and two at the podium. Captain Langely made some administrative announcements, greeted the congregation, and immediately began the items listed on the program.

"The next voices you will hear will be from our lovely, talented choir." Captain Langely stepped away from the podium. Shouts ricocheted from the microphones. There were a few seconds of silence and then a trail of harmonious voices shook the theater. I took some time to think back on a few things that had transformed me into what I am today.

God doesn't mind where we are assembled to worship Him. If we assemble ourselves then He will be in the midst.

The word "if" was revisiting my spiritual being. The big one syllable word with great power held my attention. I startled myself to know that I wasn't afraid to hear the word that was about to be rightly divided on stage. I startled myself to know that I actually *wanted* to see the boots or shoes on the chaplain. I put on my glasses to take a look at Captain Langely's boots. When he stepped briefly from behind the podium, I saw they were as mine, sandy tan. He was not the one. I still didn't understand the golden shoes and boots on certain individuals. Still, I listened attentively to the words coming from the captain's lips.

"Please give a warm welcome of praise to our choir." The captain turned and resumed his seat on the right-hand side of the stage.

The choir sang beautifully. Their voices rang like surround sound throughout the theater. I clapped and my soul rejoiced. I was truly blessed to be still breathing so many days to my departure date from the desert.

"Go back to the alter."
"Go back to the alter."
"Get down on your knees."
"Down on your knees."
"Stay there."
"Stay there 'til you get the Holy Ghost power."

I clapped and sang softly as the choir ministered in song to the large congregation. Stay there until I get the Holy Ghost power.

Minutes of praising the Lord passed and the captain returned to the podium. I looked at his boots as he approached the podium. They were still tan. I wasn't sure if I'd missed what God was trying to tell me. I felt worry rise and tried to suppress it with prayer. The captain's voice rang into the two microphones.

"Church today we have a young minister here who is going home on Sunday. He was the pastor for Camp Divers for the last year. His unit has completed their mission and they are on their way back to the United States of America. Praise God church."

The congregation clapped hard. I wondered if they knew the unit or was a part of the unit. I was relieved to know that another blessing was headed back to the United States. I clapped softly and whispered thanks to God and also asked him to bless me as well and my journey home.

"It is good that God can show us a blessing everyday of our lives. Thank God for this young minister's unit and their safe return home. Praise God. Can we show God some love this afternoon." The clapping increased as well as shouts of joy. I assumed that many of them were from the unit heading home. I thanked God once more and asked His blessing on my family and myself.

Silence stretched across the theater as Captain Langely took his seat. Minister Reeves walked up to the podium. I must have had my head down because I didn't see him until he was already positioned behind it. He stood for a few seconds before addressing the congregation.

"Thank the Lord who is the head of my life. Now saints I'm not a singer but I do want to share this song with you. Can you please help me out?" After taking in congregation confirmations, he took a deep breath and belted out the words in a deep voice. *"I need thee. Thee oh, I need thee. Every. every hour I need thee. Oh, bless me now my Savior. I come to thee."* He sang that verse about three times. I closed my eyes and swayed to the tune of his voice. The words soothed me and his voice captivated my spirit. I rocked gently and listened to Minister Reeves' song.

The song ended. I sat still ready for the next event.

Minister Reeves was a short dark skinned deep voiced serious minister. He was openly thankful for God's goodness towards him. He smiled and clapped giving all reverence to God. He even asked the congregation to join him in praising God for a few minutes. We did gladly. My soul was happy.

"Praise the Lord saints and I am indeed glad to be here standing before you today to give you what thus said the Lord."

I hadn't heard that phrase in years. I smiled and pulled out my notebook. I knew this sermon would be a keeper. I got a pen and made sure it had ink. I wrote the date in the right hand corner and waited for the minister to speak.

"Saints, I realized a few months ago that God has a condition He is setting for His people. The word "if" always denotes a condition. If you do this then I will do that. If you make good grades then you can apply for a good job. If you would humble yourself and pray then I will. The word if is powerful and is spoken with great authority."

The soldier who sat on my left spoke with the minister. She must've been familiar with God's condition or she was a part of the minister's unit and had heard him speak. After he said another sentence, I gathered she was a part of his unit.

I could feel a slight change in the atmosphere as the words of the minister flowed throughout the theater. It was a joyous yet a little weird feeling. The theater was hot when I first entered and after the beginning portion of the sermon, I felt a slight chill. I smiled and placed more attention to the sermon.

"Saints, I've notice," the minister continued, "that many of us look for truth in all the wrong places. His serious voice rang loud and clear from the front to the back of the theater. "You've heard of the song, Looking for Love in all the Wrong Places. Y'all heard that song? That's what we do church. We look for answers from folk who don't have them." He paused as the praise phrases echoed. I was amazed to hear a few originals.

"Ding, ding, ding, ding, ding," said the soldier on my left.

"Oh what ya talkin' 'bout?" shouted a soldier a few rows up from me.

"I have a reader today saints. Come on go with me to St. John 8:30. We're going to take an "if" journey throughout some of the Bible. Come on saints and stand for the Word of God. He paused again. He had a dynamic tone. I grabbed my Bible wrote on my pad and stood waiting for St. John 8:30 to be read by the reader. The reader stood diagonal of the podium. He wore civilian clothes but we all knew from his haircut that he was a soldier. He wore studious spectacles and a T-shirt with a logo on the right front and beige slacks. I could see he wore plain black shoes. They were black. I saw no gold coming from them. I immediately glanced toward Minister Reeves who stood firm behind the podium waiting for his reader. In a few seconds the command was given for the reader to begin.

"As he spake the words."

"Go head."

"Many believed."

"Yeah."

Then said Jesus, if…"

"If," Minister Reeves nearly shouted. The congregation jumped. We were still standing. "If," he repeated. The word if appears at least 1,522 times in the Bible. If. Come on reader."

"If ye continue in my word."

"If ye continue in my word. Anybody with me? The condition. What is the condition? Come on reader."

"If ye continue in my word, then ye are my disciples."

"Then ye are my disciples." The minister paused and looked about the theater. Praise phrases mixed with clapping filled the atmosphere.

"Come on reader, read on."

"And ye shall know the truth."

"And."

"And the truth shall make you free."

"And the truth shall make you free. Looking for the truth in all the wrong places. If denotes a condition. A choice. If ye continue in my word, then ye are my disciples. You shall know the truth and the truth shall make you free. See church some of us don't know the truth. We think we do but many times we just out there. Many of us don't understand the if behind the word. If, is a choice. You can, you will, or you won't."

The minister was on a roll. I listened wrote and waited for a title. Maybe there wasn't one and that was fine with me. Maybe there was one and I didn't hear it. The coolness lingered about my space. Although I sweated from warmth, I could still feel the slight chill.

"Before we go on let me tell you the title of my sermon. I know some of y'all saying okay where's he going with this. The question is Do You Know Him?" He paused as if waiting for an answer. I heard a few responses and praise phrases.

"Do You Know Him? If. There's that word again. If You Really Do, You'd do His Word. Now you can stand for the entire sermon but if you can sit then by all means do. Let me put it all together for you, *Do You Know Him?* ***If*** *You Really Do, You'd do His Word.*"

Several members immediately took their seat. I sat so that I could take better notes. A few members remained standing. I noticed the minister used the King James Version Bible. It had been a while since my deployment that I heard the word being read by a reader and from the King James Version. I glowed with excitement. I wrote "Do You Really Know Him? And in the margin I wrote the word if. I glanced up between words to see if Minister Reeves had come from behind the podium.

"I don't think you all are with me today. I don't think that many of you all know the Lord and I'm really curious to know for those who claim to know Him, *if* you really do. Let's move on with this thang here. St. John 17:14 tells us what reader?" The minister turned his head toward the reader who took in a deep breath and read.

"I have given them thy word."

"I have given them thy word. Okay."

"And the world hated them."

"And the world hated them. The world, saints, hated the word. Now why'd they hate them church? Read."

"Because they are not of the world."

"There you have it saints. They hated them and the word because they weren't of the world. Jesus disciples weren't of the world by association with Christ. But should we worry about that church? I wonder if we should worry." The minister swayed behind the podium. I wrote in my notebook and placed my attention back on Minister Reeves. I took a few glances to check to see if he'd moved from behind the podium. Didn't seem like he would and this Sunday afternoon I was ready for the golden shoes or boots. I was sure to stay attentive.

There was a short pause. I took the liberty of reading a few of the other verses in St. John 17. *I pray not that thou shouldest take them out of the world, but that thou shouldest keep them from evil.* God was still taking a chance on us even if we didn't except His word. How lovely. We couldn't ask for a better friend. A more devoted protector. I really didn't know God as well as I thought. The sermon!

"Saints if you read a few more verses in St. John 17, you'll find that God is always with us. We have obstacles everyday because the devil doesn't take a break. His job is to make you miserable." Minister Reeves spoke and flipped through his Bible. There was an added pause and another deep breath.

"The devil has a full-time job. His job is to make your life as miserable as he can. He works every day all day. No breaks. No vacations. But God is yet able. There is a way to survive those constant attacks on your life." The words rang from the front to the rear of the small church. I looked around to find my dad sitting in a corner of the church with his bible on his hand and his lead guitar under his arm. He wore a funny expression. I recognized it as something missing from the young preacher's message.

"We have trials and tribulations every day of our lives. We know those trials are the devil's work."

My dad's expression tightened. I looked at mom. She was still beautiful and she sat silently on the front sit of the small church. I was surrounded by my family waiting to hear about this survival technique. I'd been overseas for a year and half. I experienced a little of everything the devil had to offer along with every blessing imaginable from God. I'd gone from floating preachers to preachers wearing golden shoes. The devil couldn't do anything else to me that I couldn't handle with faith in God and hope of overcoming the events that created obstacles in my life.

My dad raised his head slightly. I saw the hard wrinkles in his face and knew that the preacher had perhaps unknowingly misspoke. I was surprised and a little disappointed. I was only disappointed because I didn't know what he may have missed and that my dad would probably not be pleased with the sermon. There was still a word from the Lord in his message. I listened attentively. I was just glad to be on American soil that it mattered very little. Ellery and Roesander didn't say funny things about me. I missed their wise comments but they were simply respecting my situation. I cried inside because I'd become overwhelmed with joy. I would return to this after thought.

"Saints we're going to get there. You're going to know God; I mean really know Him. Let's go to St. John16:33. It's just right next to where we left off." There was laughter in the theater. "I know some of you all pick up your bible on Sunday, blow the dust off and high tail it to service. But that's okay today saints. The Lord has a word for you even under that dust. Thank you, Jesus. Are you with me?"

The responses were happy ones.

"Ding, ding, ding, ding, ding," commented the soldier to my left. That was truly an original.

"What you say?" came from the back.

"Alright now sir," came from the middle.

The spirit was present and the chill was greater than previously. The minister stepped to the left and as I rose completely to see his feet he'd already stepped back behind the podium. My heart had leaped which let me know I wasn't as prepared as I thought I was.

"St. John 16:33. Come reader tell us what it says."

"These things have I spoken unto you."

"These things have I spoken unto you. The word of God that I have given you. The conditions of my faith. If. Come on saints we're going somewhere with this. Come on with me. Go on reader.

"That in me ye might have peace."

"That in me ye might have peace. I know He has something else to add to that. These things have I spoken unto you that in me ye might have peace. Come reader tell us what else thus said the Lord."

"In the world ye have tribulation."

"In the world ye have tribulation. Are the words in your bible red?"

Shouts of positive responses swelled the theater. I was excited to be using the King James Version.

"Okay, if. There's that word again. If your words are red then Jesus is talking to us. In the world ye have tribulation. Reader, do we have to worry?" Minister Reeves looked back at his reader. He was shaking his head.

"Tell us why we don't need to worry about tribulations. Somebody is going to get with me this evening. Somebody will. Read on reader."

"In the world ye have tribulation, but be of good cheer."

"Be of good cheer saints. Be of good cheer. Are your words still red? Yes. Jesus is telling us to be of good cheer. Oh, come on somebody! Go with me this evening!" The minister whooped and shouted into the microphone. The congregation shouted and waved their hands toward the stage. I wrote many sentences and felt a slight headache from raising and lowering my head. Partly to watch his movements and partly to have my eyes on his feet when he moved from the podium.

In this world you'll have tribulations, but be encouraged St. John 16:33. I was sure to write legibly so that I could revisit the sentence. I was happy to know that all things work together for good to those who believe on His name along with having tribulations and He still is with us. My mind was about to wonder back in time. This was *not* the time. I refocused and stayed with Minister Reeves. For many years I had a boat and I felt just like Noah and his followers. I hadn't seen the work of the Lord in my life as strong as I thought it should be. What had the young preacher missed?

A lingering thought. It was too late. I wondered once more.

The Motivator's voice sounded so pleasant on the other end. He didn't sound like we were 3,000 miles or more apart. I listened closely to hear his breathing in between sentences. I couldn't remember how long we'd been apart. Almost six months. His life was in a complete uproar trying to care for our children. We were already busy when I was at home, sharing the household responsibilities and holding a full- time job.

Many times, during deployment, I was unable to call him. The desert life sometimes didn't allow such opportunities or there were no facilities available. So, when we got the opportunity, we didn't want to waste it on trivial matters. I held the phone close to my ear. The sand storm made it difficult to hear him. I knew he was tired. It was 2 o'clock in the morning in America. He was telling me about his day at church. It'd been three years ago when God touched his life. I mean really came in and set up living quarters. I was indeed happy for his motivation and dedication to living for Christ. Although he was over fifty years old, he was a baby in Christ. He was learning all the new things I had already learned and more. He was learning and working for Christ. I listened and my heart was pleased.

"Hey Love. I went to church this evening. We had some kind of appreciation service for the deacons. It was a beautiful service." This was truly a changed man. It wasn't about how many fish he caught and when he was going back. This was about giving time to God. What a blessing.

I'm glad you got to go. You're doing so well and I'm really proud of you." I couldn't think of a word other than proud. My mom always told us not to really use that word because God was the only one who was proud. At the moment, I felt like I disrespected my mom but I was indeed very happy for the Motivator. I repeated my sentence using the word happy instead as a way to give my mom respect and remind the Motivator of my how I felt about his journey for Christ.

"I am really happy about your transformation Baby. You are doing such a great job and I'm extremely grateful. I'm also thankful for you taking care of our children." I took a breath. I wanted to hear more about him, more about his day of no fishing. I stopped talking and waiting for him to speak again. The short silence was a little unbearable. I could hear him breathing. "Are you still awake? I'm sorry it's so early."

"It's okay Love. I was just thinking."

"Let's hear it."

"At church today, there were a few members who testified. They talked about how they were on drugs and God delivered them. They talked about financial hardship, getting laid off their job and all kinds of sad things. I sat listening and thinking about how I didn't have a testimony because I hadn't gone through all those things. Then I thought I do have a testimony. I do have a good testimony." The Motivator stopped talking. I wanted to hear more. It was almost 3 o'clock in the morning on Monday. I didn't want to tell him about how I've always wanted a fiery testimony too. It wasn't my time. It was his time to shine and tell of God's goodness. I withheld for another time. The better, right time. He had to get up in a couple hours to get ready for work and get the children ready for school. He sounded so excited about his deal at church even in his tired voice I could hear the excitement. I continued to listen and say yeah and really to let him know I was listening. I was listening. I was thinking as well. I was where he was. I was there. I had no fiery testimony. I hadn't been through fire and brimstone and God bought me through. I was a blessed individual all my life. A very scary thought but God saw fit to just keep me safe for several years. I felt grateful and silently thanked God as I continued to listen to the Motivator.

My testimony," he continued, "is that I didn't have to go through all of that. I was never on drugs. I didn't have financial hardships. I have a very good job. I have a testimony, Love. God has really been good to me."

I could feel tears forming in the back of my head. The Motivator was absolutely right. We both had a testimony. God was a blessing and He'd been there for us through one mobilization after another and consecutive deployments. Now here we were thousands of miles apart, again, and when we talked the Motivator reminded me that we have a testimony. The line went dead. The sand storm decided to end our conversation. The Motivator needed to get some rest anyway.

A few weeks later I called home. The Motivator was still in good spirits regardless of his situation.

In this world you'll have tribulations, but be encouraged St. John 16:33.

The Motivator knew and understood that God would bring him through anything. He was a baby Christian. I cherished that and asked him to please not let anyone discourage him. The Motivator had a pure mind and heart. I sort of envied that. Longevity in Christ didn't amount to much. Longevity in Christ doesn't equate to wisdom and understanding of the word. It doesn't men God will use you and not the baby Christian. I learned that from my parents.

We had to live each day as if it were our last. We just don't know. Life's like a vapor. Be careful and be encouraged.

"God is with me Love and He'll make sure we make it through. He will." We had a short conversation that morning.

"I'm still in love with you. You are for me. We're going to make it."

I smiled into the receiver.

"In this world we will have hard times but all things work together for good to those who believe on his name."

I hung up the phone and pulled out my little palm size bible. I slowly turned to Isaiah 40 and read verses 28-31. I smiled and returned to work. *They that wait upon the Lord their strength shall be renewed.* The Motivator was waiting on the Lord and in his waiting his strength was being renewed.

The day's work wasn't too busy. I had a little time to recall the Motivator's heightened spirituality. I felt it. I told myself to hold on to that feeling. It would take me places.

Has thou not known?

I knew. I knew. The sermon!

I returned my attention to the minister.

The congregation was tracking by this time. The atmosphere turned from the slight chill to a bit warm. I started sweating. I looked around for a bottle of water. Maybe it was all in my mind. I could hear the congregation siding with Minister Reeves. I looked up from my writing just in time to see the minister stepping away from the podium. The golden boots blocked my sight and I think I yelped. I looked at the soldier sitting to my right. He made no indications that he saw the golden colored boots. I looked to the female soldier on my left. She made no indications as well. Instead, both of them were glued to the minister's words. I wanted to break their obvious trance and ask them if they saw what I saw. How would I ask them? I decided not to and just stared at the boots for a while and returned to writing. I'm sure I missed a few points. The stage seemed to darken and the boots appeared brighter. I pinched myself to see if I was still alive. My sweat dried quickly. I felt the chill come across my face. "What is it Lord", I tried to ask. I'd learned that God has a perfect plan and He's taken into account the events of our lives. "Why is it Lord," I'm sure I asked out loud. The sermon! I had lost track of the points.

"Come on saints and go with me to first John the third chapter. We're going to begin at verse seven. Reader when you get it, let's go." The minister wiped his forehead and motioned for his reader to begin.

"Little children, let no man deceive you."

"Little children, let no man deceive you. Now I know you're with me. Let no man tell you other than what the Lord has put out. If you believe in me then I will pour you out a blessing. That's what the Lord tells us. Unless He tells us otherwise then you have to believe that in this world you will have tribulations, but be encouraged."

Minister Reeves looked around the church. He stepped further away from the small podium. The golden boots drew my attention even though I had my head down taking notes. I readied for the chill that would strike my face in a few seconds. I wasn't as frightened this time because I was prepared. Minister Reeves continued.

"Little children, let no man deceive you. Keep on reader. What else does it tell us?"

"He that committeth sin is of the devil."

"He that committeth sin is of the devil. Oh, now didn't we know that? Some of you already did." Laughter rang through the theater. "Some of you already know you're evil.

Don't play with it." The praise phrases echoed from front to back.

"Tell it minister."

"Say it again!"

"Ding, ding, ding, ding, ding," screeched the female soldier sitting on my left. I laughed a little and watched the minister and his golden boots press on with God's word.

"Those of you who are of the devil, I got a question for you. Do you know Him? Do you know Him? First John the third chapter basically tells us that we are servants of sin. We are of the devil." The congregation grew silent. "Oh you all don't believe me? Reader, read on."

"He that committee sin is of the devil. For the devil sinneth from the beginning. For this purpose." The minister cut off his reader.

"Wait. He that committeth sin is of the devil. For the devil sinneth from the beginning. For this purpose. Now I guess God had to come do something for us. What was it? Read on reader."

"For this purpose, the Son of God manifested that He might destroy the works of the devil."

"Reader, you have got to say that again. Say it one more time for the congregation."

The reader repeated with more emphasis. "For *this* purpose, the Son of God manifested that He might *destroy* the works of the devil." Many of the members stood and clapped. The praise phrases rang across the theater.

"Make it plain."

"Say it preacher. Say it!"

I listened for the ding, ding soldier. Sure enough she said it.

"Ding, ding, ding, ding, ding." Much louder and with obvious enthusiasm.

I wrote sentences and scriptures in my notebook. I glanced to see Minister Reeves stepped back behind the podium. He wasn't coming to a close but it felt like he was. I felt the chill cross my face for the fourth time during the sermon. The golden boots sparkled like a fresh sunrise as he stepped away from the podium. I stared for moments unknown. The chill turned into a brief heat wave. I wanted to stare at the golden boots but I didn't want to miss the rest of the sermon.

"God is light. He is no darkness at all. God takes care of us because He has a covenant. He has set us up for heaven. Do you know Him?"

I only heard the blur of the last words. I hoped he'd repeat it. Instead, he went to another scripture. I tried to recall the time, as a young child, a preacher had used a series of verses to bring about a critical spiritual point. I thought my attention was captivated. I must have let go because I thought about…

The preacher stood still and looked about the congregation. He stood about six feet tall. He wore a red scarf around his neck that draped to his knees. There was a black and gold image on either end. I scooted to the edge of the pew to get a better glimpse of the images. I couldn't make them out. I watched him move very slowly. He really moved slowly. This chaplain was older than the others I had heard. He looked to be about fifty at the least. Though the years had been good to him, I could tell by his overall personality and the examples he provided that he was at least fifty.

I prepared my writing materials. There were no questions lingering in my mind. I was open to hear the word of God being rightly divided. No questions, no animosities, just a free spirit. Open minded for the reception of God's word. How long could I maintain it was the real question?

The chaplain's voice broke my trace. "In Genesis the first chapter the Lord gave out a few commands. He said let there be light and there was light. There's darkness in the world. We have to go through the darkness to get to the light." The preacher stopped abruptly. He looked about the congregation as if waiting for someone to tell him what to say next. I wasn't sure if I'd taken notice to him or took notes. Where was he going?

"How many of you are wondering, preacher, where are you going with this?" His words were stretched. He spoke like he moved. Slow. He took in a short breath and continued. Although there were no shouts of acknowledgement, the scattered praise phrases indicated that he had the congregation's full attention.

He began again in his slow voice moving his hands slowly over his bible. "Saints," a long pause and a shallow inhale, "Turn with me if you might to Genesis the first chapter. I am going somewhere with this. Bear with me."

I turned my bible pages. We had no choice but to bear with him. As slow as he spoke and moved, we had better get somewhere. I wasn't anxious but I did hope for the sake of time, I guess, the chaplain didn't read too many verses. I gave that comment a second thought and asked for forgiveness. The chaplain spoke. "In the first chapter of Genesis, beginning at verse one, we see that God created the heaven and the earth. We all know that or at least we should. But it goes on to state that the earth didn't have any beauty. So, God decided to make earth beautiful. He made light and darkness and water and land and animals and fouls of the air, and plants and trees, and all the things in the world that are good. Everything above the earth was considered heaven. Then there was something God needed to do. He separated light from darkness. He divided the day into day and night. All was good in the eyes of God." That was a lot said in a length of time. I kept focus. I wrote down the piece about the separation of day and night.

"Saints, I want you to understand where God was going with this. Let there be light He said and there was. In verse fourteen, He divides day and night and tells us that He did so to establish time frames. Verse sixteen tells us that He placed the moon, the stars, and the sun in the sky. The sun was used for the day and the stars and moon for the night. All was great and the story continues."

The chaplain moved slowly about the pulpit. I kept my attention on him. I had never looked at Genesis one and one, as did this preacher.

"So today I'm going to talk to you briefly about "Why Jesus?" Why Jesus? There is darkness in our world. We have to go through the darkness to get to the light. Why Jesus? Because of darkness we need light. Why Jesus?" I could hear a spark develop in the chaplain's voice. I wrote Why Jesus on my paper. I glanced up toward the pulpit. I decided that this sermon didn't have room for boot and shoe checking so I put my head back into my notebook.

"Why Jesus? Turn with me to St. John the first chapter. That which was from the beginning which we have heard and have seen and our hands have handled. The day, the night, the sun, the moon, and the stars. Why Jesus? Isaiah 60:1 says rise and shine the light is come and the glory of the Lord is upon us. The darkness covers the earth but the Lord and His glory makes light. Why Jesus?"

I was excited to know that Jesus was beginner and finisher of all of my days. Why Him? He was my sun, my moon, and my stars. The darkness comes but Jesus brings about a new day! I wrote in my notebook and closed my eyes to the chaplain's boots. I could feel the ray of golden light streaming from them from behind the pulpit even with my eyes closed. I recapped the statements that were spoken so soft and slow. I had time to write them almost verbatim.

"There is no need any more to question God's promises of life. Isaiah 60 tells us to lift up our eyes and see. Open up our hearts and fill up with the flowing of the seas. Be prosperous unto the glory of God for He is and will always be and was before." The chaplain paused and took in his shallow breath. I was in awe. It was all so magnificent like I was hearing it all for the first time. I wasn't hearing Genesis chapter one verse one, St. John chapter one verse one and Isaiah 60 verses one through nine for the first time. I was hearing it explained like this for the first time. Why Jesus? When the night comes the day will follow. I almost got lost in my own explanation then I heard the preacher's voice elevate slightly.

"When the night comes. Turn to Psalms 107. Take a look at verse eight. Oh!" The preacher was slowly getting excited though he continued on his slow streak I could see the spiritual excitement in his eyes. He repeated, "Oh! O that men would praise the Lord for His goodness! Move to verse ten. Sitting in darkness because ye are bound with affliction. Ye have rebelled against God's goodness. Don't. Cry out unto the Lord in darkness and guess what?" He looked about the congregation for a response. The church was sort of quiet. I could hear pages rustling in the background and I could hear whispers of praises.

"Cry out and the Lord will give you light. Why Jesus? He is the light of this world. If you go further in the verse, through the troubles of man you are reminded in verse twenty-eight to cry out unto the Lord and in verse thirty-one, Oh!!! That men would praise Him for His wonderful works He has done for His children. Why Jesus? That's why." The preacher swayed in the middle of the pulpit. The church was in a quiet uproar in a good way. The darkness of the church was peeling away as slow as the preacher spoke. I wrote almost verbatim in my notebook. I could feel tears of joy swelling up in the back of my head. Why Jesus? Because when the night comes, we can't see. When the night comes, we get confused. When the night comes, we work our evil in the darkness. But, if we cry out, then the Lord will show us the light. Praise Him for His continuous works of wonder! I must have shouted out loud. I was happy. I picked up my pen from the floor. The chaplain was moving behind the pulpit. I smiled in his direction and continued to listen.

I could tell the preacher was going to take a new twist but keeping with the same topic. I turned to a fresh page and wrote the date in the corner. I realized I had no name for this fabulous preacher. He didn't wear an Army uniform and I didn't recall hearing his name. I pulled out the folded program. The name of the speaker was Master Sergeant Gowan. Master Sergeant. I wrote MSG Gowan under the date on the fresh page.

"Why Jesus? Turn with me, if you can stand it, to St. John 3:16. Our classic scripture." I was familiar, as was many of the members, with John 3:16. I knew the answer to this portion of why Jesus. I flipped quickly to St. John the third chapter and went straight to the sixteenth verse. I moved my lips slowly as Master Sergeant Gowan spoke the words loud and slow.

"For God so loved the world that He gave His only Son to die for the sins of the world. He gave His Son as light to the people who were trying to live out their life in the dark. St. John 3:16 takes us to the personal level of why Jesus. When we learn to swim, we have to trust the waters. We can't stay in the shallow parts of our faith. We have to take a chance and launch out into the deep. If you feel like you're drowning, there's something you can do." The pause was longer this time. I kept my eyes glued on his.

"When you sit in a chair, you trust the weight. Labor in the night because joy is in the morning. Why Jesus?" There was another long pause.

"Do you know Him? Come on saints you have to stay with me." I returned my attention. I wasn't sure if I'd missed much of Minister Reeves' sermon.

"We're going now to I John 1:5-9. God is light. He is no darkness at all. If we say God is darkness, we lie. Reader, tell us what it says."

"But who so keepeth his word, hereby know that we are in him.

"He that keepeth his word knows that God is in us. Go on."

"He that saith he is in God will walk in His ways."

"Those whose light shines we know they are of God. Yeah."

"And he that says he is in the light and hate his brother is still in darkness."

"Now come on you all. If, you say. Oh, here we go if. If you say, "I'm in the light" and hate your brother, you are still in darkness. Do you know Him?" Minister Reeves smiled at the congregation. I smiled at my copious notes. I was taking it all in and loving it. I was also wonder how to use it. Lots of scriptures to cover one point: Do you know Him?

"You got to be running with the "in crowd" saints. God knows we ain't right. God is light. There is no darkness in Him. None at all. If we say there is darkness in those who believe on Him, we lie saints we have just lied!" Mom didn't like us using the word "lie" or "liar". Wonder what she'd think of his word choice. I listened.

I felt like a master writing down the scriptures and periodically glancing up at the pulpit. Minister Reeves had stepped from behind the podium. The entire theater lit up like a Roman candle! Light shone everywhere. I looked at the minister. His face looked much lighter than the beginning of the sermon. I held onto my scream. I checked my notes and wrote a few more points.

The minister continued. "Turn with me to St. John 1:1 and 14. The reader is going to tell you something else. And then I'm going ask you again." He pointed into the congregation. Someone got the message because they responded, "Do you know Him?" I said nothing. I did however write down the scripture. There were several scriptures referencing this topic. I wrote St. John 1:1, 14 on my new page. I put an asterisk by the number one. I was familiar with St. John one and one. In the beginning was the Word and the Word was God and the Word was with God. What I wasn't getting was the tie in of this scripture to the text. The reader belted out the first verse.

"In the beginning was the Word."

"In the beginning was the Word. Now I know you all knew that. Walk with me. Come on reader."

"And the Word was God."

"And the Word was God. The Word of light was God. The maker of darkness as a time of day was God. Read on. Somebody is going to get it before it's all over. Read on. Verse fourteen."

The reader took a few breaths and cleared his throat before speaking.

"And the Word was manifested in the flesh and dwelt on earth with us. And we beheld all His glory."

"The Lord was made flesh and lived on earth with us. We saw Him. But, do you know Him?"

I was still on track. The minister began with the word if. He was still on the conditions of Christ's love. There are three that are on record in heaven, The Father, the Son (Word) and the Holy Spirit. All are one. So where are we? What is our state? I must have left my listening to the minister. I put my attention on something in my past.

"Do you know the Lord?"

The choir and Praise Team did an excellent number for the congregation. This evening was the first Sunday without Chaplain Groct. I didn't want to have favorites when it came to the Word of God so I cleared my mind. I prepared for the Word as I'd done all the other Sundays. I was however in a fabulous mood concerning my position in Christ. I was keeping the faith and being thankful in the midst of every situation. I watched the coconut skinned medium height chaplain approach the podium. I immediately checked his boots since he was in uniform. I thought it awkward but I'd already looked. There was no blaze of gold peering from the pulpit. I swallowed in fright more than disappointment. It was an awkward but necessary move. I asked for forgiveness and readied my notebook, Bible and pen. I didn't put on my glasses and hoped the chaplain would give his name. I pulled out my announcement program to look for it. It wasn't there. I was sure to put my best attitude forward and give all thanks to God.

"Praise to all saints. My name is Chaplain Sherdon Clogic. I arrived in theater two months ago and was ministering at Camp Case just south of here. I am very happy to be here. I look forward to ministering to you, with you, and watching those chosen grow in Christ as ministers." His voice sounded like a thick southern accent and he giggled between sentences. I took this as a habit; a part of his personality.

"I think I'll be with you for the next six months. You think that's enough time to give praises to God?" He giggled, as the congregation seemed to take right to him. I smiled at their immediate show of respect. He was only a Lieutenant Colonel but that didn't appear to be what was important to him. He was more concerned about the presence of the Lord. I smiled at him. He didn't see me but the presence of the Lord felt it.

"Well, this is my first sermon. My first sermon on this camp." He giggled again. I'd get used to it and tune it out as background noise. His thick curly hair made him look younger than his probably forty-five years. His smooth coconut skin barely wrinkled when he smiled. There were very few smile wrinkles in his face. I could tell the years had been good to him. He had a deep voice that echoed when he spoke. I thought it sounded magnificent. He wasn't a terribly large man but he wasn't too skinny either: just the right size. He placed his Bible on the small podium and stared out into the congregation. I assumed he was taking it all in. We waited for a few seconds.

"Have you ever wondered why some people are healed and others seem like they aren't? Do you ever wonder why some people get sick or die before reaching their destiny?" He looked out into the congregation. That was a loaded statement! I tried to keep my spirit up and my mind focused. I'd been down that path before with God and I wasn't ready to take that trip again, ever again in my life. It seemed too painful. But I'm supposed to have grown since then. I'd resolved immediately yet reluctantly that Chaplain Sherdon Clogic. I needed to hear this today. I'd gotten to the point where I was thankful and encouraged and was keeping the faith and placing myself where God needed me to be. Now this, why do some people get healed and others don't? Did I want to know? No, but I surely needed to *understand* why. I wrote it in my notebook. I waited for the next words from the preacher of the hour.

"Turn with me to Isaiah 53:4 and 5." The pages turned. The pages sounded anxious as they turned. I think mine's turned the fastest and with a greater degree of anxiety. I tried not to act too anxious and I prepared myself for disappointment. When I got there, I started reading. *Surely he hath borne our grieves and carried our sorrows. He was wounded for our transgressions. The chastisement of our peace was upon him and with his stripes we are healed.*

"If you're there say amen. Today I want to use for my text "The Healing Passion of Christ". We have to realize that we are just dirt. Piles of dirt. Actually, we're not even dirt. We're dust. The problem is that one pile of dust thinks it's better than the next pile. When it comes to us going through remember that Jesus died so that we could be healed from our past. So why is it that some of us are healed and others are not?" The preacher with his coconut skin took a step to the front of the podium. This time I refused have my mind entangled with his boot colors. Instead, I looked upon his Godly features. He was handsome in a spiritual way. I didn't see that when he first walked into the pulpit. I was glad to have been more observant this time. He placed his hand on the edge of the podium and giggled. "Turn with me to St. John 10:10." More giggling as the pages flipped. He must have already had his Bible to the page or knew the scripture by heart because he didn't move position. The silence of the congregation felt weird for some reason. I could hear the chaplain giggling a little. He giggled once more and spoke.

"In St. John the tenth chapter we see that Jesus is speaking to man. The red writing lets us know that." He giggled. I wasn't sure if he was joking or if it was his habit. I didn't laugh though I found the comment quite amusing.

"I am come that ye may have life more abundantly. I am the good shepherd who gives life to his sheep. So that, saints, tells us that we are healed. Turn with me to Matthew 26:26."

St. John 10:10 and Matthew 26:26. How ironic. I turned my Bible to the said scripture and read it before he announced if all had it.

"Now here we see that the Word of God is addressing His people. Jesus is also speaking here. Jesus took the bread blessed it and broke it saying take eat this. It is my body. Now turn to Acts 3:1-12. As a matter of fact, you should read that entire chapter. Here we see that a man who was born a cripple was healed in the eyes of man by the grace of God. He rejoiced and people saw the great miracles of Christ. The people were praising Peter. "Oh no man. I didn't do this," Peter told the crowd. God does heal and He is merciful and gracious. What about Mark the sixth chapter? Let see what thus saith the Lord there. Turn with me please to Mark 6." The preacher then moved from position and returned to the back of the podium. He pressed on the breast pockets of his uniform. I could hear pages turning, comments being made, and souls were probably rejoicing. Along with that I could sense a few confused hearts. Mine was perhaps one of the many. I turned to Mark the sixth chapter and began reading immediately.

"A prophet is not welcomed by his own but a stranger will befriend him readily. How sad. Jesus came unto His own and His own received Him not. Why are some of us healed and others aren't? We'll wait to answer that for you. I have two more and we'll move on. James the fifth chapter. Let's see what the Word says concerning the healing passion of Christ." I could still hear him giggling under his breath. I wrote the scriptures in my notebook. I wrote a few key words to trigger my memory when he came to the wrap up of all the points.

"Let's begin at verse seven. Be patient brethren and wait for the Lord. Remain patient and don't grudge against one another in your wait. Be patient and wait for those who endure shall be happy. Now I Corinthians 11:23-26. We'll go there and see what the Lord has to add. You should be there by now."

I hoped I didn't detect a bit of an attitude in Chaplain Sherdon Clogic's voice. Maybe I was a bit testy in anticipation of the answer to the question.

"For I have received the Lord. And that night He took bread and broke it and commanded us to eat of His body and drink of His blood to show reverence until He returned. We're earth suits of dust living on the promises of Christ Jesus. We're no better than the next pile of powerless dust. And you ask why do some people get healed and others don't? I must've lost time somewhere while going back in my time.

"You know those folk who like to run with the "in crowd". You know the ones who have to dress like the Jones. We all have come across someone who will knowingly do wrong and then ask God well what about me? Oh yes y'all going with me today. Y'all going to get this message." This was the voice of Reverend Dolle. His voice rang strong across the oversized church. I counted twenty people and the message sounded like it could've been for twenty thousand people. Yet and still Sunday after Sunday Reverend Dolle preached the word of God to twenty. Sometimes less. As the deploying units moved into the hot zone the crowd got smaller but Reverend Dolle's spirit was fresh every Sunday. The Reverend Dolle stood only 5 feet 4 inches. His was charcoal black and smelled like an All-American football player. He wore a light green pimp strip suit this Sunday. I really wanted to laugh because pimp stripes were so out dated back in the states. Pimp stripes had been out of style for a while but he made them look like the greatest fad in fashion. I also didn't think Reverend Dolle cared. For the four months he was on my camp I'd only seen him on Sundays in a colorful suit. Last week he wore a bright baby pink suit with a yellow shirt. He gave the Word of God to the people with spirit and grace. I turned over my program and wrote the date in the corner. I'd forgotten my notebook in my haste.

"Why we got so many people running in the opposite direction of where Christ wants them?" He snatched the cordless microphone off its stand and headed out into the area where we sat. I smiled and waited in wonderment for his next words. "Why? Let me tell you. Because we are the devil. That's why. Oh, y'all don't hear me. Some of y'all offended already and I only been up here for five minutes. Your skin is thin and your heart ain't right. Yeah, I said it and I have proof. Go to St. John 8:44. Some of y'all ought to know this verse real well." He squinted his face and appeared darker. I laughed and waved my hand in the air. I don't usually do that. I surprised myself with what looked normal to others. I turned my Bible to St. John 8:44 though I already knew the verse. My dad explained this to me years ago. He would use this verse many times to explain a point. He was eliminating my excuses to think I had a right to question God's plan, to think I was actually better than someone else. I remember him telling me that maybe I wasn't better than somebody else. Now here stood the short and happy Reverend Dolle about to tell me for the umpteenth time.

"Ye are of your father the devil. That's right. And whatever your daddy tells you, you gonna do. He was a murder from the beginning and had no truth. There was no truth in him and he wasn't looking for any truth anyways. When he opens his mouth, lies come out. His own lies. That's because he's a liar saints. And you are a part of him if you don't believe in Christ Jesus. Oh no I didn't just use the word if. Yes, I did. We gonna get back to that word. Now. You all devilettes and devilees you practice sin everyday doing what yo' daddy tells you to do. Then when you take ill, you skip work and head down to the Troop Medical Clinic to fix you. But you know you sinning. You even do it on the base. You know you have to write a good check to cash at the PX. You know you need a Kevlar when you in the HUMMV. You know you not supposed to be in mixed uniform. You know you not supposed to spoke in housing. But what do you do? You do it anyway. You willfully sin and then want God to step in. You know you suppose to tell the truth but you lie instead. You know you supposed treat people with dignity and respect but you discriminate. You know you supposed to help those in need but you make excuses. Now go to I John 3:9. Get on to that scripture so we can get her done."

The praise phrases rocked the church from one side and Reverend Dolle rocked to the other side. He spoke too fast and with that thick Southern accent that I stopped writing and just listened. He was absolutely right. About all of it. Then we wonder why others are healed and some of us aren't. I was going to get that question answered before I got back to America. I went to the verse as instructed. Read a bit and waited for the Reverend.

"Yes, yes, yes look at what it says. He that is born of God does not commit sin because God's seed is in him and he cannot sin. But those who love not their brother and who do not accept the seed, guess what? You ain't righteous and you commit sin. Now go to Hebrew 10:26 and see if we can't clean ourselves up a little. Come with me now." The pages turned and the praises rocked the chapel. It was indeed an awesome sermon. I didn't remember him saying a title. I got to Hebrews ten and began reading.

The Reverend burst in, "Now if we sin after we done got the word, we ain't got an excuse. There aren't any more excuses. We sit here and hear the Word of God. We know what we need to be doing. Do we do it? No. Okay. Okay go to Exodus 19:5 because I think some of y'all trying to get out of what I just said. You probably right now trying to concoct an excuse. Come on go to Exodus 19. Anybody need help finding it?"

The congregation of about twenty sounded like a multitude of disciples. God never worries about numbers. He only needs one. Hands waved, ministers stood, and I soaked it all in because he was talking too fast for me to write.

"Oh snap, snap, snap, snap. Look at what this tells us. If you will obey the voice of the Lord. If. There's that big ole word that we don't even like. If you will obey my voice and keep my commandments. Some of y'all gon' be hurt cause y'all got two things to do. Obey and keep, oh snap. If you obey my voice and keep my word, should I say, then y'all aren't of the devil any more. Y'all are my own and since I own the earth, I can save you. The Lord is going to bless your comings in and your goings out. Isaiah 40:28-31 simply tells us to wait. No matter what happens, wait. Just obey my voice and keep my commandments and wait. If you wait upon the Lord, He shall renew thy strength. Now why are there those who are healed and others who aren't? Ask them about their power source. Ask them where do they plug up for energy when theirs have been drained from trials and tribulations. If you obey and if you keep my commandments then you can plug in and I will give you the power you need to go on."

That was the answer. I needed power from the source and the source is Jesus. I need to put the plug in the right place. I almost shouted that Sunday. The power source of Christ is what will keep us when we feel like death dried up. Dried up bones. Plug into the power source.

The short Reverend closed his Bible and closed his mouth. He came from behind the podium and set the chapel on flames with his golden shoes. The green suit was even brighter. He smelled and looked divinely handsome. I lifted my eyes in an effort to suck up His very presence. I plugged into the power source to strengthen my dried bones.

Chapter Eleven

The Power Source

It had been a long tour of duty. I was coming to the end of it all and was certain to get home in much better spiritual, mental, and physical shape than over a year ago when I left the United States. I stood on the sidewalk watching the sunrays play on the barriers that lined my building. I was thanking God for all of His blessing He's given me.

I'd left my building early today to get a good seat in the theater. I was glad to see that the seventh row was wide open. It was amazing to see how many troops had come as early as I had. Usually, the church fills up and then there are many sitting on the floor and in the aisles. A couple of Sundays ago, the preacher announced that the ushers could no longer make extras rows. It was said to be a fire safety. So, I decided to get to church a few minutes early to get a good seat.

I went to the seventh row and sat on the third seat. I closed my eyes and said a short prayer asking God for forgiveness, thanking Him for continued grace and mercy and asking Him to please watch over my family. I really needed Him for at least 90 more years at the least.

The church was filling up fast after 2 o'clock in the afternoon. By two fifteen, the head chaplain took his place at the podium. He praised God and had the congregation praise Him as well. We praised Him and I'm sure He came right in and occupied several hearts, minds, and souls. The Sunday was beautiful and I was on my way home very soon. I was purposely looking for something to help me through my transition from out of the desert to America, to my home. I needed something powerful from the Lord through the servant of His choosing.

I pulled out my notebook and Bible. I checked three pens to get a good one. I couldn't get comfortable. Perhaps I was tired for working such long hours last week. I'd worked all last night but I wanted to hear this last sermon of the desert. I had completed my "boat" and wanted to know when would I have to use it.

A boat in the desert.

Someone asked me earlier what was the significance of a "boat in the desert". I was more than happy to explain. We need health insurance. Although we may not be sickly, we need to have good health insurance. It only takes one time for your child to break his arm. It only takes one time for your daughter to get pneumonia. Then we really need our health insurance because we may not be sick at the time or feel it's necessary. The same goes for the Fire Department. A firefighter works for twenty-four hours. While he's at the job, he may not have any calls. That's good. You may see something different. You may see a team of twelve men reporting to work and surfing the Internet and reading magazines. But oh, don't let a major fire break out. They need to be ready. For if it's ever a time the fire department isn't ready someone is going to be unhappy. If ever you have to pay a lump sum health bill, you'd wish you had paid into health insurance. Having insurance is peace of mind when a crisis happens.

Same goes for the ark that Noah was instructed to build. Yes, the people laughed at him but Noah trusted God. All that desert. All that sand. There was no rain. There was no need for a boat in the desert. There is no need for God when things are going well. In the eyes of the unbeliever, unnecessary stuff is their mantra. In their minds, there could've been no way it would have rained. It hadn't rained in years. I pay health insurance every month and I've only been to the clinic for an annual check-up. I worked for the Fire Department. I've seen them stay on shift and not have a single call. Yet I still paid into insurance. Yet every day a new shift of firefighters reported.

It never rains in the desert. But the people were wrong. God promised rain. It would be rain. When the rain came, Noah was very ready. So why a boat in the desert? Why have a boat in your desert of life? To be ready. To stay ready. You just never know.

Now why is it that we can't find our place in Christ? Why is it that we can't seem to stay encouraged? Why is it that we need evidence to be faithful to God? Why is it that many of us still don't really know who Christ is? Why is it that we question having a boat in the desert?

This Sunday, my last Sunday in the desert a lady told me through ministry in words.

The female Department of Defense (DoD) civilian walked up to the theater pulpit. She moved with added purpose. Though she wore an Army uniform, I knew she was a civilian employee because she wore her cherry red hair down her back and draped over her thin shoulders. She looked spiritual but not aggressively so. I smiled and arranged my items. The congregation stood when she locked in behind the pulpit. She hadn't even asked. Her voice was deep and confident. She didn't wear rank on her collar. She did have a DoD nametape on her uniform. She pulled open her Bible and looked out at us. I pulled out my program to get her name. It wasn't there. Maybe she was a surprise. Maybe the scheduled speaker had an emergency. She touched what I assumed was her Bible and began to pray. The congregation on cue went with her to God. Heads bowed, hands raised, eyes closed. Her voice was soft and gentle yet strong with authority. She cried out to God on our behalf. She must have known something we didn't know. The hands waved and the saints prayed. We were on one accord with God that afternoon. The prayer was short yet powerful. "Amen Lord," she ended softly. "Amen."

The minister didn't have a reader like Minister Reeves. Her voice was filled with experience and I knew when she began reading that she didn't need a reader.

"I went to Joy Night last night. How many of you were there?" Hands went up all over the theater. Not sure why that question was asked but I went along with it as it may connect somewhere. Well, I'm not Minister Reeves, but he spoke on dry bones. There an was attractive congregation who got an ugly ear full of what's wrong with us and what we need to do to progress as Christians." The congregation suddenly hushed. The silence could have sliced butter. The minister's captivating voice held the congregation in positive suspense. The congregation seemed to suddenly grow extremely attentive.

"I don't know if I told you my name," she began rather calmly. I am Minister Governor. I come today giving thanks to God for wetting and watering my dry bones. See Minister Reeves preached on dry bones last night. And since it appears from the polls that many of you missed it, I'm going to bring it to you again because I feel like this is something you need to hear. For your reading pleasure, I'm taking my text from Ezekiel 37:1-10." The point was made and connect. I put on my active listening gear. I now needed to make sure it worked for the entire sermon.

I wrote down the scripture and looked up at the podium. For the first time I noticed that the podium was slightly raised and I could see her tan colored boots from where I sat without even moving. They were just plain boots. I was startled or disappointed. Not sure which at the moment. I was eager to learn about these dry bones. I retuned my attention when I heard her voice.

"And he asked Lord, can these bones live? And I answered thou knowest. Then he said prophesy to the bones and tell them to hear the Word of God. He did and God put breath into him. Then he took the bones and flesh came upon them and then he put breath inside the flesh to show that he was God. And then all the bones were stood up and given life thus creating a strong Army. God put life into those dry bones that were laid across the desert. He put power in them and they lived."

Minister Governor stepped in front of the podium and surveyed the congregation. The congregation remained attentive and standing. I wrote a few phrases. The church was almost absolutely silent.

"Ezekiel 37:1-10 saints and I'm going to take the title "Are You Plugged into the Power Source?" She repeated. "Are You Plugged into the Power Source?" Minister Governor looked at the congregation while she pinned up her cherry red hair. I figured she wanted to be ready for her powerful message. No obstacles in the way of the word and the witness.

She put the finishing touches on her newly formed bun and continued.

"Dry bones, are you plugged into the power source of Jesus?"

The congregation seemed to have suddenly come alive. Praise phrases shattered the silence.

"Make it plain preacher."

"Tell it, tell it!"

"Say that preacher!"

"Okay let's look at it this way. You know when you haven't paid your bill and you think all is good? You go to your apartment and you see this big red sign on the door that reads DISCONNECTED! You have been unplugged from your power source. You ride around town in your Excalibur and it comes to a halt in the middle of the street. You check the fuel gauge to see that you have no gas. You have been unplugged from the power source. Even better you talk on your cell phone for minutes, you surf the internet and you stream videos for hours. Then one day you have an important call to make and the nice lady on the other end says, "I'm sorry but your service had been discontinued". You have been unplugged from the power source." The minister took a breath and the congregation grew a bit louder. The praises were all over the theater. I wrote and listened closely. These were good points.

The minister stepped toward the choir. She was able to move freely about the stage because she wore a pin on microphone. We were able to hear her anywhere she stood. She flipped her Bible waved her hands and continued bringing the word.

"Ezekiel 37:1-10 tells us that the dry bones were lifeless and someone wanted to know if they could live. Only God knew if and God knew how. So, He said tells the bones that they will live. Tell the bones I will breathe life into them. You have to pay your rent in order to keep living in your apartment. You have to keep a full tank of gas to keep driving. You have to pay your cell phone bill to keep texting, talking, internet surfing, and live streaming. And most of all saints, you have to be a child of God to survive in the world. God is our power source and I want to know are you *plugged* into it?"

It was all coming to me now. Nice and clear and connected. Our life is just like the activities of the world that keeps the world in worldly motion. Behind every heavy rain fall there's a rainbow. At the end of every electrical appliance plug is a power socket. Now I know we have gone wireless over the years, but yet and still that has a power source. Also, for every moving vehicle there's fuel and even the electric vehicles have a power source. For every flickering light there's a bulb. I knew that God loves me and I needed to be encouraged. I understood that I needed to be thankful in the midst of my storms. I even trusted that God would make a way for me always but I neglected to practice staying plugged into the power source. Every moment of darkness I've experienced and couldn't find my way out I had pulled the plug. The times I couldn't see God's grace and mercy, I had pulled my plug. For all those times my peace was slipping, I may have gone too far away from my power source. Even if I have the plug, it has to reach. I'd better get back to Minister Governor. I was supposed to be practicing good active listening skills!

The church was on fire. They'd probably plugged in their power source after realizing it was disconnected. The minister went on with her message.

"Saints our lives are like the disconnections we see every day. Many of us have experienced those very terminations of services. And the sad part is that some of us didn't realize or won't admit that we pulled our own plugs. Remember saints we don't have to be in the dark. Christ tells us that if you love me, keep my commandments. Stay plugged into the power source. Saints, we don't have to struggle. If you feel left out in the cold, check your power source. Behind that storm is a rainbow just like at the end of that cord is a socket. Everyday isn't a happy day." She paused as if thinking of her next point. She pressed to check her cherry red bun. It was still tightly pinned atop her head. She touched her Bible and moved toward the ministers on her right. I watched her every move. I decided to absorb this sermon. I needed to get my power source, plug in and stay plugged. Active listening!

"Saints, let me tell you and you know it's true. Every day isn't a happy day. It is a condition, however, in which we should be thankful. We ought to rejoice in all we do. How many of you have laptops?" Hands raised everywhere. "And you sometimes operate without the power cord. Am I right?"

"That's right. Make it plain,"

"We're still with you."

"Say it preacher."

"Now as soon as that light starts flickering telling us our battery is low, what do we do? We grab that cord and plug it in. We travel with the power cord even if we don't plan to use it initially. We just want to have it with us just in case. We need to take Jesus along with us too. Just in case. Back to that laptop. Now some of you have warning signs. The laptop tells you, you're at 20 percent power. Please plug into power. Something of that sort. As soon as you see that message, you plug in. Christ is the same. You can plug Him in everywhere and any time." She moved away from the ministers and returned to the podium. I'd raised my head in time to see the golden boots appear from under the raised podium. "I know," I yelled out. The soldier sitting next to me asked me was I alright. I wanted to tell him to look at the preacher's feet but I was too frightened. I stared but was sure to continue to listen carefully.

"Saints, when that battery on the laptop runs low and you plug in your power cord, it's okay. Just like it's okay to tell people you're struggling. It's okay to have a bad day. It's okay. The dry bones were bought to life and you can be bought to life over and over and over and over again. Just, saints, remember that God loves you. Be thankful in the midst of your trials. Be forever encouraged. Know God. I mean really get to know how truly awesome He is. Know where you are in Christ and have faith without physical evidence. Be patient and do well and know that the good of the Lord is your power source. And if you do nothing else…stay plugged into the power source of Christ."

A boat in the desert was the power source for Noah. He was prepared to plug in when the storm and flood came. He stayed faithful and trusted God when there was no rain. The people laughed and teased and refused to believe that there was need for a boat, in the desert. Like life insurance, Noah built. Like the firefighter, Noah built. Like the laptop off the battery source, Noah built. And sure enough, one hundred and fifty years later, God flooded the earth. Noah simply plugged into the power source and all who believed with him were saved.

"If you do nothing else, stay plugged into the power source of Christ."

Amen.

Epilogue

Coriander Scottsville returned home after more than a year tour in the Middle East. She was determined to use what she'd learned from the many soldiers who impressed her and those whom she left a mark of love. Today, she tells those who love Christ that life is like the boat Noah built in the desert. That huge ark that would be his power source. People laughed and thought it would never have any use. Noah continued to build. Keep your charger at the ready. Have your charger with you at all times. Know where those electrical sockets are located so that you can get to them. Build your boat in the desert so that you are ready for the flood.

Living for Christ is just like that boat in the desert. We think we have days when we don't need God to guide us so we go about that day thinking we've survived it on our own. We think that we don't need God because we left home with power at 100%. Chargers get left in places out of our reach all the time. Electrical outlets don't always produce electricity to get more power or to completely charge. But oh, like the preacher said, if ever we get unplugged from the power source, we are only steps away from safety. Build your boat no matter what the people say. Keep your power cord close and plug it in!

God loves us dearly and will do all He can to keep us happy and safe. But...

What If God Didn't Love Me?

Christ died for us so we could live long and better days.
He bore the cross for many of us as we
dwelled in our worldly ways.
I challenge you to ask yourself, "What if God didn't love me?
What if He never gave His Son to
die so that I could be free?"
What if God didn't love us? What if God didn't love me?

Christ protects us as we live our lives
daily; going to and from.
As I sit and reminisce of how much life is worth,
I thank God for His Only Begotten Son.
I ask again have you asked yourself
"What if God didn't love me?"
I must admit that I am glad where I am right now.
For if He didn't love us, without Him where would I be?

God loves the world now as He loved it then
Though we still saturate our lives with sin.
The shedding of His Son's blood was where His love began.
What if God didn't but good thing He does.

Remember God loves you.

We have no worries because He does.
Thank you again reader for taking the time to listen.

Printed in Dunstable, United Kingdom